WARS OF EMPIRE
IN
CARTOONS

Also by Mark Bryant

*Dictionary of British Cartoonists and
Caricaturists, 1730-1980* (with S. Heneage)

*Dictionary of Twentieth-Century
British Cartoonists and Caricaturists*

World War I in Cartoons

World War II in Cartoons

God in Cartoons

The Complete Colonel Blimp (ed.)

The Comic Cruikshank (ed.)

Vicky's Supermac (ed.)

Nicolas Bentley (ed.)

H. M. Bateman (ed.)

WARS OF EMPIRE
IN
CARTOONS

Mark Bryant

GRUB STREET • LONDON

For Robert and Julius

First published 2008 by
Grub Street Publishing,
4 Rainham Close, London SW11 6SS

Text, translations and picture selection © Mark Bryant 2008

British Library Cataloguing in Publication Data

Wars of empire in cartoons: Crimean War, Indian Mutiny,
  Afghanistan, Zulu War, Sudan, Boer War
  1. Great Britain – History – 19th century – Caricatures
  and cartoons 2. Great Britain – Colonies – History –
  19th century – Caricatures and cartoons
  I. Bryant, Mark, 1953-
  941'.081'0207

ISBN 978 1 902304 40 3

Design by Roy Platten, Eclipse.
roy.eclipse@btopenworld.com

Printed and bound in Singapore

Madam England:
'The world belongs to me, the others can have the rest.'
Alfred le Petit, French cartoon, c.1900

CONTENTS

PREFACE

THIS BOOK TAKES a similar approach to its companion volumes, *World War I in Cartoons* and *World War II in Cartoons*, in that it is intended primarily as a pictorial history of the period as seen through the eyes of the cartoonists and caricaturists who lived through it and chronicled the events as they occurred. In this case the period is the nineteenth century and the wars of the British Empire during the reign of Queen Victoria from the Crimean War to the Boer War when she was succeeded by Edward VII. As with the earlier books, I have added some historical background to link the images and help put them in context and, where possible, I have also supplied some information about the artists themselves and the publications (many of them now long forgotten) in which the drawings were originally published. In addition, I have once again tried to include material from both sides of the conflicts involved but, as before, this has been limited somewhat by considerations of time and cost. Also, as in the previous books, the main emphasis has been on political and joke cartoons published in national newspapers and magazines, though material from other sources, such as books, prints, postcards and posters, has also been included.

In the preparation of this book I am indebted to Nick Hiley and Jane Newton of the British Cartoon Archive at the University of Kent, the St Bride Printing Library, the British Library, the British Newspaper Library, the Senate House Library of the University of London, the London Library, the Goethe Institute, the Institut Français and all those listed in the acknowledgements at the back of the book. Last, but by no means least, my thanks also go to John Davies, Anne Dolamore, Hannah Stuart and all at Grub Street Publishing for all their support, and to the designer Roy Platten, for producing such a handsome book.

Mark Bryant
London, 2008

"IF THEY WILL IRRITATE HIM THEY MUST TAKE THE CONSEQUENCES."

INTRODUCTION

IN AN ESSAY published in 1932, Winston Churchill admitted that he had loved political cartoons since his childhood, adding that they were 'a very good way of learning history'. However, for those brought up on computer-generated animation, graphic novels, children's comics, *manga*, Batman, Superman and the multifarious works of Disney et al., historical wartime cartoons may come as a bit of a surprise. They may also be unaware how far back such graphic satire reaches. For not only was there a wealth of material produced during the First and Second World Wars by artists on both sides of the conflict but a considerable amount also appeared during the wars of the British Empire in the Victorian era.

When Queen Victoria came to the throne in 1837 it seemed that the sun would never set on the vast global empire that Britain had built up using her industrial power and mighty navy since the fall of Napoleon. This British 'golden age' found expression in the splendour of the 1851 Great Exhibition in London, then the largest city in the world, and the massive 165-vessel review of the Royal Navy at Spithead, Portsmouth, in 1897 – the most impressive display of warships ever seen. However, the 'Pax Britannica' created by the 19th century's dominant superpower was not all that it seemed. The forces of Her Imperial Majesty were frequently called upon to fend off aggressor nations which threatened British interests – especially the 'Great Game' played out with Russia over India, the 'Jewel in the Crown' of the British Empire – and to quell rebellions in Britain's many colonies using 'gunboat diplomacy'.

The Crimean War against Russia was the only major conflict in Europe involving Britain in the 100-year period that extended from the end of the Napoleonic Wars in 1815 to the beginning of the First World War in 1914. The other main wars of the British Empire took place in Asia and Africa – the Indian Mutiny, the Opium Wars with China, the Ashanti and Zulu Wars, the Afghan Wars, the Wars in Egypt and the Sudan, and the Boer War in South Africa. All were featured in cartoons by British artists as well as by those working for the nation's allies and opponents.

As in the First and Second World Wars, the impact of cartoons and caricature was considerable. As Churchill said later in the article mentioned above, 'they have great power indeed, the cartoonists', and added that it is frequently through cartoons that ordinary people get their opinions: 'On these very often they form their views of public men and public affairs; on these very often they vote.' And he ought to know, as he lived through many of Victoria's wars. Not only did Churchill serve in India, Egypt and the Sudan but he also took part in the famous charge of the 21st Lancers at Omdurman in 1898 and made a dramatic escape from a prison camp during the Boer War. Indeed such was his fame that even before he first entered Parliament after the so-called Khaki Election of 1900 the 27-year-old was caricatured for *Vanity Fair* magazine in its 'Men of the Day' series.

It should be remembered that the wars of the British Empire took place not only long before the invention of the internet and the modern computer, but also before television, radio, cinema, the telephone and even (at the beginning) the international telegraph – and the motorcycle, automobile and the aeroplane only came at the very end of this period. This meant that news was very slow to reach the public and it was only during the Crimean War that the first war correspondents, war photographers and frontline war artists of any kind began to appear. Added to which, daily and weekly newspapers were only printed in black-and-white and very few carried any illustrations at all, let alone cartoons. Of the few British newspapers that did, many no longer exist, and none of the surviving upmarket national publications from this period – such as *The Times, Sunday Times, Observer,* and the *Daily Telegraph* – published any cartoons or caricatures until the 1960s.

The word 'cartoon' (from the Italian *cartone*, meaning a sheet of paper or card, from which we also get the word 'carton') was originally used to describe designs or templates for tapestries, mosaics or fresco paintings, but its more widely used modern sense derives from a *Punch* spoof by John Leech of a competition for decorating the walls of the new Houses of Parliament in 1843. Classical-style cartoons sent in for the competition were exhibited in Westminster Hall and Leech attacked this as a waste of public money at a time when Londoners were starving, and headed his drawing 'Cartoon No.1'. Thereafter, the main weekly full-page topical drawing of the magazine was referred to as 'the Cartoon' and the word gradually came to be applied to comic or satirical drawings generally.

The art form itself, of course – together with that of caricature (from another Italian word, *caricare*, meaning to overburden or exaggerate) – has a long history going back to Ancient Egypt, but it became increasingly popular from the 18th century onwards with the works of Hogarth, Gillray, Rowlandson and the Cruikshanks and such overseas masters as Ghezzi, Chodowiecki, Philipon, Daumier, Wilhelm Busch, and others.

However, though cartoonists had chronicled the Napoleonic Wars in political and satirical prints (often hand-coloured) it was with the arrival of more widely available specialist journals containing cartoons and caricatures in the mid-19th century – led by *La Caricature* (1830) and *Le Charivari* (1832) in France – that their impact really began to be felt by all sections of society. By the beginning of the Crimean War (1854) the long-lived George Cruikshank (one of the young star cartoonists of the Napoleonic Wars) was still producing occasional political prints (he died in 1878) but the most influential group at this time were the artists of *Punch*. Founded in imitation of *Le Charivari* (its full title was *Punch, or the London Charivari*) it began on 17 July 1841 during the First Opium War and the First Afghan War and soon dominated the international cartoon scene. It was followed by *Fun* (1860), *Judy* and *Moonshine* (1867) and *Vanity Fair* (1868) in Britain; *Fliegende Blätter* (1844), *Kladderadatsch* (1848) and *Simplicissimus* (1896) in Germany; and *Puck* (1876) and *Judge* (1881) in the USA – among many others worldwide.

The abolition of the 'taxes on knowledge' (advertisement, stamp and paper duties) by 1861 made a huge difference to the availability of the printed word (and picture) in Britain, and the Education Act of 1870 meant that ever-increasing numbers of people could now read. As a result, by the outbreak of the Boer War in 1899 a large number of new daily and weekly newspapers – as well as magazines – had begun to appear. Many of these published regular caricatures and/or topical and political cartoons either by their own artists or by arrangement with other journals. They included *Ally Sloper's Half Holiday, Daily Mail, Daily Express, Daily Graphic, Daily Chronicle, Daily News, Graphic, Illustrated London News, Morning Leader, Pall Mall Gazette, St Stephen's Review, Sketch, Strand Magazine, Tomahawk, Western Mail* and *Westminster Gazette*. Amongst their overseas rivals were *L'Assiette au Beurre, Figaro, Le Grelot* and *Le Rire* (France), *Jugend* and *Lustige Blätter* (Germany), *Amsterdamse Courant* and *De Amsterdammer* (Holland), *Delhi Sketchbook* and *Indian Punch* (India), *L'Asino* (Italy), *Novoye Vremya* (Russia) and *Harper's Weekly* (USA).

With all these publications came new cartoonists. In Britain these included John Leech, John Tenniel and Linley Sambourne on *Punch* (and even a young Bernard Partridge who would still be working through the First World War and almost up to the end of the Second World War), Gordon Thomson (*Fun*), William Boucher (*Judy*), Phil May and Tom Merry (*St Stephen's Review*), David Wilson (*Daily Chronicle*), Arthur Moreland (*Morning Leader*), J.M.Staniforth (*Western Mail*) and 'Ape' and 'Spy' (*Vanity Fair*). Amongst the notable foreign cartoonists of the period were Gustav

Brandt and Ernst Retemeyer (*Kladderadatsch*), Thomas Heine and Bruno Paul (*Simplicissimus*), Leal da Camara, Charles Léandre and Jean Veber (*L'Assiette au Beurre*), Honoré Daumier and 'Caran D'Ache' (*Le Charivari*), and Thomas Nast and W.A.Rogers (*Harper's Weekly*).

The wars themselves produced plenty of opportunities for humour: new 'ironclad' ships and 'Long Tom' guns, the red coats and bearskin hats of British troops (and the kilts and bagpipes of Scottish regiments), and garishly dressed foreign soldiers (whether Zulus, Ashanti, Indian, Chinese or Sudanese). However, a number of Victorian cartoons would not seem so funny today. Not only did many have long-winded captions but the topics themselves would be less acceptable in the 21st century. Sexist and racist jokes were common – especially those attacking Disraeli's Jewish ancestry or portraying Africans as music-hall 'nigger minstrels'. There were also many cartoons relating to class consciousness, such as those making fun of cockney street urchins, washerwomen, costermongers and farm labourers. Naval and military cartoons, by contrast, tended to favour the ordinary soldier and sailor, with many lampooning aged generals and admirals or supercilious young 'drawing-room captains' who had bought (rather than earned) their commissions.

Personal caricature also featured widely. As with the Napoleonic Wars the main protagonists – whether royalty, politicians or military leaders – were frequent targets for the satirist's pen, and many were a gift to cartoonists: Boer President Kruger with his top hat, long beard, pipe, umbrella and Bible; British Colonial Secretary Joseph Chamberlain with his monocle and white orchid buttonhole; King Kofi of the Ashanti drawn as a coffee plant (or with a coffee-pot on his head); the diminutive Lord Roberts; the 'old woman' Prime Minister Lord Aberdeen; the overweight Edward VII; the extravagantly moustached Napoleon III; and the fastidiously dressed Disraeli.

As there was no conscription in Britain during this period, very few professional cartoonists saw frontline action. However, a number of serving soldiers drew cartoons, notable examples from the Boer War being Colonel Robert Baden-Powell (hero of Mafeking and later founder of the Boy Scout movement) and Captain Clive Dixon of the 16th Lancers who was aide-de-camp to General White during the siege of Ladysmith. And at least two important artists established their reputation during the wars of the British Empire. John Tenniel of *Punch* achieved his first major success with his Indian Mutiny cartoon 'The British Lion's Vengeance on the Bengal Tiger' (1857), which was reproduced as a very popular print (Churchill later described it as a 'lovely cartoon'). And the most successful caricature ever drawn by Leslie Ward ('Spy' of *Vanity Fair*) was his portrait of Lord Roberts (1900).

Cartoonists on both sides also produced advertising posters and postcards. However, I have concentrated mainly on newspaper and magazine cartoons in this graphic scrapbook of the wars of the British Empire for the simple reason that these would have been the most widely available to the general public. The only difficulty here, though, is that by their very nature newspaper cartoons are ephemeral and the publications they appeared in were usually thrown away by the following day. Hence the present compendium which, it is hoped, will preserve some of them for posterity.

THE CRIMEAN WAR

THE CRIMEAN WAR was the only major European conflict involving Britain between the end of the Napoleonic Wars and the beginning of the First World War – that is, in the 100 years from 1815 to 1914. Fought between Russia and the allied forces of Turkey, France, Britain and later Sardinia, it began when Tsar Nicholas I of Russia, an Orthodox Christian, claimed the right to protect Christians in the Holy Land which was then part of the crumbling Ottoman Empire ruled by Muslim Turkey. Despite Turkey being described by Nicholas as the 'sick man of Europe' its ruler, Sultan Abdul Medjid, rejected Russia's claim and thus the Crimean War began as a Russo-Turkish war.

The first actions were Russia's occupation of the Turkish vassal states of Wallachia and Moldavia (now Romania) on the River Danube and the destruction of the Turkish Fleet at Sinope on the Black Sea coast. Seeing the threat to the Turkish capital of Constantinople (modern Istanbul) the allied forces of Britain and France then joined Turkey, declared war, and attacked Russia's main Black Sea port of Sebastopol on the Crimean peninsula. After bloody battles on the Alma River and outside Sebastopol at Balaklava (including the famous 'Thin Red Line' and the Charge of the Light Brigade) and Inkermann – and the death of Tsar Nicholas – the Allies eventually prevailed and the war ended with the Treaty of Paris on 30 March 1856. The Crimean War was also notable for the work of two pioneers in their fields – the nurse Florence Nightingale and the first ever war correspondent, W.H.Russell of *The Times*.

A Good Joke
Russian: 'Oh, it's my fun! I only want to frighten the little fellow.'
John Leech, *Punch*, 23 July 1853

In June 1853 French and British fleets were sent to Besika Bay, off the Dardanelles, to protect Istanbul and Turkish shipping and as a warning to the Russians not to attack the Ottoman Empire. Then on 2 July 1853 Tsar Nicholas I sent troops across the Russian border to occupy the Ottoman vassal states of Wallachia and Moldavia (the so-called 'Danubian principalities' which later merged to form a new state, Romania). These principalities bordered Russia, the Austro-Hungarian Empire and the Ottoman Empire and Russia claimed it was entitled to occupy them under the Treaty of Adrianople signed after the Russo-Turkish War of 1828-9. Turkey disagreed. To try and avert war a conference was held in Vienna between Austria, France, Prussia and Britain, and the resulting proposals – the so-called 'Vienna Note' – were sent to Russia and Turkey. However, neither country accepted them and three months later, Turkey gave Russia an ultimatum to evacuate the Danubian principalities within 14 days. When Russia refused, Turkey declared war on 4 October and on 23 October sent troops to the area under the command of Omar Pasha (a former Austrian soldier who had converted to Islam).

In 'A Good Joke' (*left*) by John Leech (1817-64) in *Punch*, France and Britain (in navy uniforms) protect the tiny Turkish Sultan, while in 'Consultation about the State of Turkey' (*below right*) the two doctors examining the 'sick man of Europe' are the new Emperor of France, Napoleon III (nephew of Napoleon I), and British Prime Minister Lord Aberdeen while hovering above the Sultan is the deathly figure of the Tsar (holding a knout in his left hand). 'Turkey in Danger' (*above right*) was the first major animal drawing for *Punch* by John Tenniel (1820-1914), later to achieve fame as the illustrator of Lewis Carroll's *Alice in Wonderland* (1866) and to become the first cartoonist to be knighted.

Turkey in Danger
John Tenniel, *Punch*, 9 April 1853

Consultation about the State of Turkey
John Leech, *Punch*, 17 September 1853

A Bear with a Sore Head
John Leech, *Punch*, 26 November 1853

At the Battle of Oltenitza (4 November 1853) – ancient Constantiola – in what is now eastern Romania at the confluence of the Danube and Arges rivers, the Turks under Omar Pasha won their first victory over the Russian Army in more than a century. However, their joy was short-lived as on 30 November the Russian Black Sea fleet completely destroyed a Turkish squadron of seven frigates and three corvettes at its base at Sinope on the north coast of Turkey, drowning 4000 Turkish sailors. The harbour and its fortifications were also destroyed. This action caused great indignation in Britain and France which was aggravated still further when the pious Tsar attended a *Te Deum* service (a service of thanksgiving featuring the hymn *Te Deum Laudamus* – We Praise Thee, God) soon afterwards. As a result Britain and France sent their fleets from the Dardanelles into the Black Sea itself on 3 January 1854 and quickly dominated the area as the Russian fleet was mostly obsolete and it had no large steam-powered, screw-driven ships. Also, on 9 February the Duke of Newcastle, the British Secretary of State for War, issued orders for 10,000 troops to be sent to Malta (the Royal Navy's main base in the Mediterranean) from where they could be quickly deployed to defend Constantinople. The British public wanted revenge despite the peace-making manoeuvres of Prime Minister Lord Aberdeen.

Imperial Piety!
or the Russian *Te Deum* for the Successful Slaughter at Sinope
George Cruikshank, 1853

Te Deum!
John Leech, *Punch*, 28 January 1854

In Leech's cartoon (*opposite, top left*) the Russian bear's sore head is a result of having been hit by a Turkish cannonball marked 'Oltenitza' and the following cartoons by Napoleonic War artist George Cruikshank (1792-1878) and Leech attack what is seen as the Tsar's religious hypocrisy. In Cruikshank's drawing (*opposite, bottom left*) note the explosion with bodies and a ship's mast in the background, while Leech (*opposite, bottom right*) has the Tsar (with vampire bat wings) playing the *Te Deum*. In 'St Nicholas of Russia' (*right*) the Tsar's halo is made from bayonets and he wears a mortar crown.

'What It Has Come To' (*below*) shows peacemaker British Prime Minister Lord Aberdeen fighting public opinion in Britain as he tries to hold back the British lion while the Russian bear runs amok.

Saint Nicholas of Russia
John Leech, *Punch*, 18 March 1854

What It Has Come To
Aberdeen: 'I must let him go.'
John Leech, *Punch*, 18 February 1854

13

The Bear and the Bees – A New Version of an Old Story
John Tenniel, *Punch*, July 1853

**The Fogs of the Danube or
the Russian Nightmare**
Gustave Doré in *La Sainte Russie* (1854)

**'Damn!...It was really stupid of me to want
to take on the whole of Europe'**
Honoré Daumier, c.1854

The United Service
John Tenniel, *Punch*, 4 March 1854

The British saw the Russian actions as a threat to Constantinople and thereby British interests in India, while Napoleon III of France (who had become emperor in 1852) needed military glory to shore up his fragile régime at home. As a consequence, on 12 March 1854 Britain and France – sworn enemies 40 years earlier when Wellington faced Napoleon at Waterloo – formed an alliance with the Ottoman Empire. Soon afterwards Britain and France sent a joint ultimatum to Russia to evacuate the Danubian principalities by April or face war. The Russians refused and on 27 March France declared war on Turkey's side, followed the next day by Britain. In addition Austria gave political support to the Allies. The Crimean War had now begun in earnest.

These cartoons depict the Allies' view of Russia. In 'The Bear and the Bees' (*opposite, top left*) the Russian bear is trying to steal the honey (note the beehive shape of the Blue Mosque of Constantinople in the background) but is attacked by Turkish bees (left) and others brandishing flags of Austria, Prussia (both neutral but by the Conference of Vienna pledged to guarantee the integrity of Turkey), France and Britain. 'The Don and the Windmills' (*below, right*) has a similar message with Turkey as the mill and its allies as the sails. Nicholas is seen as Cervantes' fictional character Don Quixote, the foolish old soldier who tilts at windmills with Baron Brunow (Russian ambassador to London) as his side kick Sancho Panza. 'The United Service' (*opposite, bottom right*) has British and French soldiers as allies with a common foe 40 years after the Napoleonic Wars (this cartoon was very popular in Britain and was reproduced many times, even decorating the backs of playing cards). In 'Right Against Wrong' (*top right*) the figure of a resolute-looking Britannia is seen holding an unsheathed sword and carrying a battle standard with the British lion ready to pounce. In the French cartoon (*opposite, bottom left*) by Honoré Daumier (1808-79) the Tsar, dressed in military uniform, is shown losing his balance – as well as his cap – when the globe rolls back over him as he tries to grab the Danubian principalities with his right hand. In the other French cartoon (*opposite, top right*), by Gustave Doré (1832-83), the nightmare mists that appear above the Russian troops are French soldiers.

Right Against Wrong
John Leech, *Punch*, 8 April 1854

The Don and the Windmills
John Leech, *Punch*, 18 March 1854

Fellow-Feeling – The Bombardment of Odessa
Aberdeen: 'Bombardment of Odessa! dear me, this will
be very disagreeable to my imperial friend.'
Nicholas: 'Bombardment of Odessa! Confound it!
This will be very annoying to dear old Aberdeen.'
John Leech, *Punch*, 13 May 1854

Not a Nice Business
John Leech, *Punch*, 1 July 1854

Another Russian Victory!!!
See the 'Invalide Russe'
John Leech, *Punch*, 8 July 1854

The Giant and the Dwarf
Giant: 'Well done, my little man!
You've drubbed the Russians at Silistria –
now go and take Sebastapol.'
John Leech, *Punch*, 5 August 1854

After their declaration of war at the end of March one of the first actions by the Allies was the shelling of the Russian Fleet by frigates of the Royal Navy at the Ukrainian Black Sea port of Odessa to the west of the Crimean peninsula in April. Then on 26 May an Anglo-French force occupied Piraeus harbour near Athens to prevent the Greek Navy joining Russia against Turkey (Russia had backed the Greek Orthodox Church's claim to protect the Christian sites in Palestine). In June the Allies sent an Anglo-French force of 55,000 to Varna, a fortified seaport on the Black Sea in Bulgaria (which had resisted strongly during the Russo-Turkish war of 1828-9). However, on 14 June Austria signed a treaty with the Ottoman Empire agreeing to occupy the Danubian principalities and in August the Russian forces, under General Mikhail Gorchakov, withdrew. None the less the Russians continued to besiege the Turkish Black Sea fortress of Silistria (in modern Bulgaria). Begun on 20 March 1854 the siege continued until 22 June 1855 when the Russians under Field Marshal Ivan Paskievich eventually retreated, having lost some 10,000 men and with Paskievich himself wounded.

Britain at this time had been ruled since December 1852 by a Conservative-Whig (Liberal) Coalition government under Prime Minister George Gordon, the 4th Earl of Aberdeen, which also included Lord Palmerston (Home Secretary) and Lord Russell (Foreign Office) from the Whigs and Gladstone (Chancellor) from the Peelite Tories. At first the reluctance of Aberdeen to engage in hostilities with Russia gave rise to accusations of his being pro-Tsar, as can be seen in 'Fellow Feeling' and 'Not a Nice Business' (with Aberdeen polishing the Tsar's boots) from *Punch* (*opposite, top left and right*). The cartoon from July 1854 (*opposite, bottom left*) shows a Turkish soldier chasing Tsar Nicholas I of Russia who is weighed down by a cannonball labelled 'Silistria'. (The *Invalide Russe* or *Russki Invalid* ['The Russian Veteran'], 1813-1917, was the Russian Army's daily paper based in St Petersburg and was well known for its phoney war reports.) 'The Giant and the Dwarf' (*opposite, bottom right*) shows Lord Aberdeen as one of the two heads and French Emperor Napoleon III as the other while the caricature of Nicholas I (the Colossus of the North) by Frenchman Alcide Lorentz (*right*), shows troops holding the Turkish flag about to cut off his nose while British soldiers trim his nails and others look on.

The Russian Colossus
Alcide Lorentz, July 1854

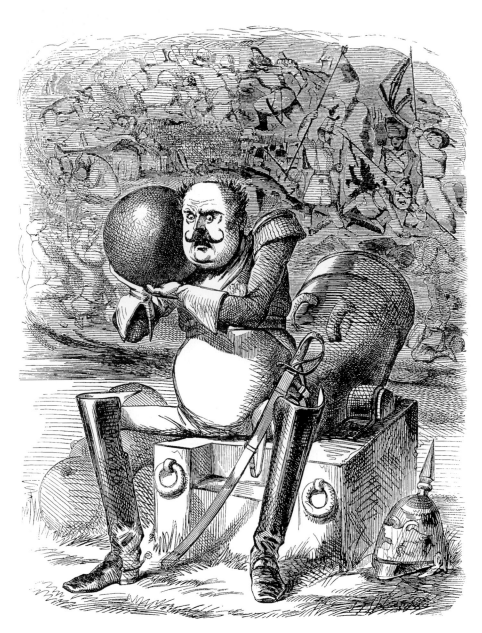

What Nicholas Heard in the Shell
John Tenniel, *Punch*, 10 June 1854

After evacuating from Varna the Allied expeditionary force of 62,000 landed unopposed in Kalamita Bay near Yevpatoria (Eupatoria) on the western side of the Crimean peninsula, 30 miles north of Sebastopol, on 14-15 September. It consisted of c.20,000 British infantry and cavalry under the command of the one-armed 65-year-old Lord Raglan (he had lost his arm at Waterloo), c.40,000 French infantry of the Army of the Orient under Marshal St Arnaud, and additional troops from Turkey. As the Allies advanced south on their objective, Sebastopol, they were opposed by 36,400 Russians under Commander-in-Chief General Prince Aleksandr Menshikov and General Gorchakov who were in a strong defensive position on the Alma River. The Battle of the Alma took place on 20 September. The Allies crossed the river, stormed the heights and beat the Russians. The British losses were 362 killed and 1621 wounded, the French lost 63 killed and 560 wounded, and the Russians lost 1800 killed and 3700 POWs (many of whom were wounded). This first Allied success left the road to Sebastopol open. The war, they thought, would be over in a matter of weeks.

In the *Punch* cartoon by John Leech (*left*) the artist has Nicholas sitting on a mortar and listening to a cannon's shell as he would a sea-shell. (Invented in 1827 the original shells were spherical, like cannon balls, but were hollow and packed with explosive. They later became cylindrical.) What Nicholas hears is conjured up in the cloud behind his head and is bad news for Russia (note that the drawing has been transposed from the artist's original as the word 'Freedom' appears in reverse on the pennant to the left of the cannonball). The same message comes through (*opposite, top left*) in Leech's allusion to Mary Shelley's novel *Frankenstein, or the Modern Prometheus* (1818) which suggests that Nicholas has created a monster (with cannons for legs and a mortar for its body) that will eventually destroy him. 'Victory of the Alma' (*opposite, top right*) shows British, French and Turkish soldiers saluting their conjoined colours while the third drawing (*opposite, bottom*) has Nicholas exploding (note the gloves marked 'Irresistible Power' and 'Unlimited Means').

The Russian Frankenstein and his Monster
John Leech, *Punch*, 15 July 1854

Victory of the Alma
John Tenniel, *Punch*, 14 June 1854

Bursting of the Russian Bubble
John Leech, *Punch*, 14 June 1854

Allies Catching Cold
Russian cartoon, 1854

Evening Party at Sebastopol
John Leech, *Punch*, 4 November 1854

Scene: A Bedroom in Sebastopol
Old Gentleman (who is rather deaf and very sleepy):
'Somebody knocking at the door – COME IN!'
John Leech, *Punch*, 9 December 1854

After the Battle of the Alma, the Allied advance stopped for three days due to exhaustion and sickness. (The French commander, Marshal St Arnaud, caught cholera – not a cold as in the Russian cartoon [*left*] – and died soon afterwards on 29 September, being replaced by General François Canrobert, nicknamed 'Bob Can't' by the British.) As a result the Russians had a considerable amount of time to regroup and to improve the fortifications of the huge and already well defended naval base of Sebastopol. Eventually, three days later, 60,000 Allied troops marched south. Deciding not to attack the by now highly fortified north of the city, they looped around it to the east to begin a southern assault, setting up supply bases at the ports of Balaklava (British) and Kamiesch (French). Then, with naval domination of the Black Sea, they laid siege to Sebastopol on 28 September 1854 (a siege which would last almost a year, until 8 September 1855). The siege began with a huge bombardment and also included shelling by the Royal Navy from the Black Sea. Already blockaded, the Russians decided to scuttle their fleet in the harbour to avoid capture and to reinforce their defences.

In their first attempt to break the siege of Sebastopol, the Russian General Liprandi decided not to attack the entrenched Allies dug in around the city but instead led 25,000 men of his field army in an attack on the British supply base near Balaklava, a seaport town on the southwestern coast of the Crimean peninsula, eight miles southeast of Sebastopol. The plan was to cut off the British Army from their supplies. The 1st Battle of Balaklava took place on 25 October 1854. After defeating Turkish forces defending the Causeway Heights, 3000 Russian cavalry of the Kievksi Hussar Regiment No. 11 were halted by a much smaller force – 550 men drawn up in a line two deep – of the 93rd Highlanders (later Argyll & Sutherland Highlanders) commanded by Sir Colin Campbell and dressed in red military jackets and kilts. In the words of a report by *The Times* war correspondent W.H.Russell: 'The Russians dashed on towards that thin red streak tipped with a line of steel.' They were subsequently known as 'The Thin Red Line' and were immortalised by Kipling in his 1892 poem 'Tommy' ('But it's "Thin red line of 'eroes" when the drums begin to roll...').

After being halted by Campbell's Highlanders, the remaining 2000 Russians were then driven back by a spectacular charge by the 900 sabres of the 4th Dragoon Guards of the Heavy Brigade under Brigadier James Scarlett (one of very few British soldiers of rank to have attended university – Eton and Trinity College, Cambridge). For this he was promoted major-general and later commanded all the cavalry in the Crimea.

The Battle of Balaklava also saw the courageous but disastrous Charge of the Light Brigade. Confused messages from Lord Raglan to Cavalry Commander General Bingham, 3rd Earl of Lucan, led to the suicidal attack by Lucan's brother-in-law, Brigadier James Brudenell, 7th Earl of Cardigan, against 30 Russian guns in a well-defended pass. The brigade rode 1¹/₂ miles down a valley at the guns while also being attacked by artillery on both sides. Of the 673 horsemen who rode in – bravely led from the front by Cardigan himself – only 198 returned unscathed and most of the horses were killed or had to be destroyed. The French general Pierre Bosquet witnessed the charge and remarked: *'C'est magnifique mais ce n'est pas la guerre...'* ('This is magnificent, but it is not war'). The incident was also made famous in a poem by the Poet Laureate Alfred Lord Tennyson published in the *Examiner* on 9 December.

A Trump Card(igan)
John Leech, *Punch*, 25 November 1854

Enthusiasm of Paterfamilias, on Reading the Report of the Grand Charge of British Cavalry at Balaklava
John Leech, *Punch*, 25 November 1854

After defeating the Russians at Balaklava the Allies continued to bombard Sebastopol with devastating effect. The anonymous French cartoon (*left*) has Tsar Nicholas' head being blown off by a cannonball as he is being shaved. Meanwhile, the Daumier and Doré drawings (*below*) both have Nicholas as a hot-air balloon that is running out of gas – in the Daumier one he has been punctured and floats to earth where thousands of bayonets await him, while Doré has him trying to reach the moon (on which sit the Allies, surrounded by clouds of Allied ships. A Russian soldier is saying 'Sire, sire, you are losing all your gas'.

French cartoon, c.1855

The Northern Colossus
Honoré Daumier, c.1854

Gustave Doré in *La Sainte Russie* (1854)

The Battle of Inkermann (Sunday 5 November 1854) was another attempt by the Russians under their Commander-in-Chief Prince Menshikov to break the Allied siege of Sebastopol. A force of some 57,000 Russian troops with more than 200 guns launched a double attack on the 8500 British holding a ridge near the Tatar village of Inkermann near Mount Inkermann on the eastern extremity of Sebastopol harbour. At first the battle – which was fought furiously by both sides – went the Russians' way against the hugely outnumbered British and the dying words of the English General Sir George Cathcart were 'I fear we are in a mess'. However, with the arrival of a French division under General Pierre Bosquet the tide was turned and the Russians were eventually defeated after particularly fierce encounters at Sandbag Battery. At the end of the battle Bosquet exclaimed *'Quel abbatoir!'* ('What a slaughterhouse!'). Out of 8500 British troops c.2300 were lost (killed or wounded). The French lost c.1000 out of 7000 but the Russians came off worst, losing 11,000 out of 35,000 men.

These two *Punch* cartoons by Leech comment on the fact that, at the request of the Russian Commander-in-Chief Prince Menshikov, Tsar Nicholas had sent his third and fourth sons, Grand Duke Nicholas (then 23 years of age) and Grand Duke Michael (then 22), to take part in the Battle of Inkermann.

The Russian Bear's Un-Licked Cubs, Nicholas and Michael
John Leech, *Punch*, 25 November 1854

The Czar to His Cubs
Czar: 'Welcome, my children; Inkermann is a glorious victory for you.'
Cubs: 'Ah Sire, if that is victory, we should like to have a defeat the next time!'
John Leech, *Punch*, 2 December 1854

The British government was attacked in the press for its poor conduct of the war – especially regarding the organisation of transport and medical services and the incompetence of generals such as Commander-in-Chief Lord Raglan. The Prime Minister Lord Aberdeen came in for special attack and was even accused of being pro-Russian. These two savage cartoons send a clear message. In the first one the wheel spells out the word 'Government' (and note Aberdeen's tartan stockings and coronet over his sou'wester). Shortly after publication of the second drawing, where it is suggested that Aberdeen is sent out to the Crimea to work as a nurse, he resigned following a vote of censure in Parliament.

You are requested not to speak to the man at the wheel
John Tenniel, *Punch*, 24 August 1854

How to Get Rid of an Old Woman
John Tenniel, *Punch*, October 1854

It should not be supposed that everyone was in favour of the war. There was also a strong peace movement led by the Manchester-based MPs John Bright and Richard Cobden – who had won widespread support as leaders of the Anti-Corn Law League which had eventually resulted in the abolition of the unpopular Corn Laws in 1846.

In the first cartoon Bright, right, and Cobden give the spoilt child Tsar Nicholas, who has already smashed his drum and other soldiers, a toy Turk to play with. In 'A Bright Idea' the militaristic British lion – representing popular opinion – thumbs his nose at Bright who wants to put him in chains.

Pet of the Manchester School
'He shall have a little Turk to pull to pieces – that he shall.'
John Leech, *Punch*, 15 April 1854

A Bright Idea
John Leech, *Punch*, 22 April 1854

The Queen Visiting the Imbeciles of the Crimea
John Leech, *Punch*, 14 April 1855

In 1855 Queen Victoria and Prince Albert toured hospitals in Britain that were looking after the sick and wounded invalids of the Crimean War. *Punch*, which was highly critical of the inefficiencies of the British Army, has the Queen and Prince Albert visiting the 'imbeciles' of the Crimea which it called 'a class of sufferers, if not as numerous, at least as severely afflicted', in the hope that reforms can be made. (The reference to green coffee is to the fact that unroasted coffee beans were sent out to the troops, making them useless.)

John Leech, *Punch*, 11 November 1854

The official total number of British deaths in the Crimea was 18,058. Of these only 1761 died from enemy action. The rest – 16,297 – died from disease (and of these 13,150 died in the first nine months), including cholera, because of bad sanitation and improper clothing etc. The death rate from disease in the French Army was much lower. The appalling conditions in the British hospitals reported by William Howard Russell and Thomas Chenery in *The Times* horrified the public at home (the French military hospitals were far better). As a result, in November 1854 Florence Nightingale (1820-1910), Superintendent of the Hospital for Invalid Gentlewomen in London, acccpted an invitation from her friend, War Minister Sidney Herbert, to take a contingent of 38 nurses to the region and supervise the British hospital for the wounded (an old Turkish barracks) in Scutari (modern Uskudar) across the Bosphorus from Contantinople (Istanbul). Thanks largely to her efforts in imposing strict hygiene and cleanliness deaths from cholera, dysentery and typhus fell from 50% to 2%. She was known as 'the lady with the lamp' because she allowed no other nurses than herself to attend the wards at night (when they were manned by orderlies). She later became the first woman ever to hold the Order of Merit (1907).

Many cartoons played on her name, as can be seen in those shown here. The 'jug' of the nightingale is a pun on the sound the birds make (see Keats' 'Ode to a Nightingale').

The 'Jug' of the Nightingale
Punch, 25 November 1854

The Real *Invalide Russe*
John Leech, *Punch*, 22 July 1854

**The Emperor (With the Mild Eyes)
Objects to the Naked Truth**
John Leech, *Punch*, 11 November 1854

In Britain there was very little press censorship at this time.
However, when things began to go wrong for the Russians,
censorship was imposed, as is shown in the two *Punch* cartoons by
Leech. (Note the Turkish soldier leaving the Tsar's sick room and
the fact that not only is Truth being clothed by the Tsar in the lies of
the Russian military paper *Invalide Russe* but also a large candle
snuffer is being placed over her head.)

Our War Correspondent
'Ape' (Carlo Pellegrini), *Vanity Fair*, 16 January 1875

William Simpson
The Baillie, 1874

The Crimean War was the first war to be reported widely in the national daily press in Britain, and the first official independent civilian war correspondent at the front was W.H.Russell (1820-1907) of *The Times* who actually witnessed the events as they happened. Before Russell the British press had either copied war reports from foreign newspapers or had used reports from army officers sent back from the front. Born in Tallaght, Co. Dublin, Ireland, he became a reporter in 1841 and arrived in Gallipoli in the Dardanelles on 5 April 1854. Within a very short time his critical dispatches from the front line began to be published in *The Times* (then the largest selling daily paper in Britain – in 1852 its circulation was 40,000 copies a day, its nearest rival's was only 7000). These caused widespread concern about the conditions of British troops and the conduct of the war. It was Russell who is credited with the phrase 'the thin red line' (he actually wrote 'the thin red streak tipped with a line of steel') in his account of the Battle of Balaklava, and his criticisms of the sufferings of the British Army in the freezing winter of 1854-5 led indirectly to the fall of Prime Minister Lord Aberdeen and the removal of the British Commander-in-Chief, Lord Raglan.

After the Crimean War Russell went on to report on the Indian Mutiny, the American Civil War, the Franco-Prussian War, the Sudan, the Zulu War and many other conflicts. He also founded and edited the *Army and Navy Gazette* (1860) and was knighted in 1895.

The Crimean War was also the first conflict in which newspapers employed 'special artists' to draw scenes at the battlefront. Amongst these were Joseph Archer Crowe of the popular weekly *Illustrated London News* (founded in 1842 and which by then had a circulation of c.200,000). Crowe had been recommended to the editor by Thackeray, himself also a cartoonist and writer for *Punch* who resigned from the magazine that year over a number of issues, including a cartoon of the French Emperor as a Beggar on Horseback 'galloping to hell with a sword reeking with blood'. The *ILN* also employed Edward Goodall and another artist at the front was William Simpson (shown here in a caricature from the Glasgow-based periodical *The Baillie*), who produced paintings of the war for a series of lithographic prints.

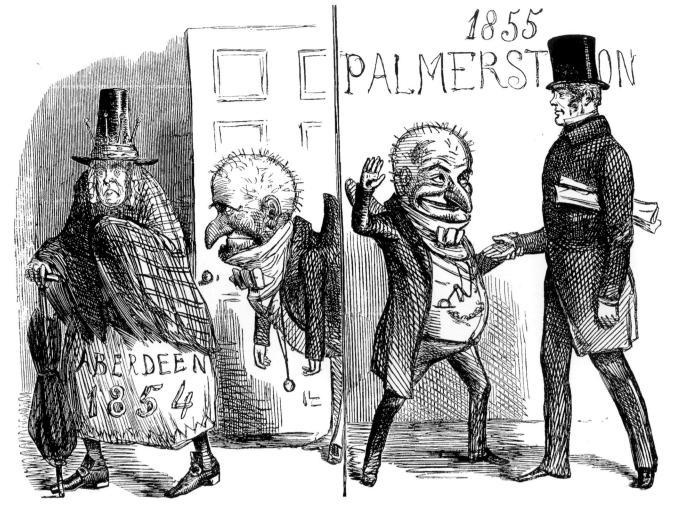

Seeing the Old Year Out and the New Year In
John Leech, *Punch*, 6 January 1855

Now for It!
A Set-to between 'Pam the Downing Street Pet'
and 'The Russian Spider'
John Leech, *Punch*, 17 January 1855

Despite a particularly hard winter in the Crimean Peninsula (the snow was three feet deep in Balaklava), 1855 was a good year for the Allies. The first positive note was sounded in January when King Victor Emmanuel of Sardinia (later king of a unified Italy in 1861) and his prime minister, Count Camillo Cavour, joined the Allies and agreed to send a division (15,000 men) to the Crimea under Alfonso, Marchese di La Marmora, an Italian who entered the Sardinian Army in 1823 and was Minister of War 1848-59 (his brother Allessandro, who died while serving in the Crimea, created the famous Italian light infantry known as the *bersaglieri*). Then in February the Independent radical MP John Roebuck (a friend of J.S.Mill) attacked the government in Parliament and his successful motion to appoint a committee of inquiry into the conduct of the war led to the resignation of Lord Aberdeen. As a result the popular, 70-year-old pro-war former Home Secretary Viscount Palmerston – seen by some as the Winston Churchill of the Crimean War – was appointed as prime minister of a Liberal government on 10 February 1855. Public confidence in 'Pam' and his new Secretary for War Lord Panmure (succeeding the Duke of Newcastle) was high – as is shown in these two *Punch* cartoons – and most expected a speedy end to the war.

Soon after the appointment of Palmerston as British Prime Minister an attack on the Crimean seaport of Eupatoria by 40,000 Russians under their Commander-in-Chief General Gorchakov was defeated by the Turks at the Battle of Eupatoria (17 February 1855). This was followed by the death of the Tsar, who succumbed to pleurisy on 2 March 1855 and was succeeded by his son Alexander II. On 18 June the main Allied attack on Sebastopol began, led by the French under their new Commander-in-Chief General Aimable Péllissier (Canrobert having resigned due to ill health and disagreements with Raglan). The attack failed through lack of sufficient artillery support.

'"General Février" Turned Traitor' (*right*) is perhaps one of the most famous cartoons of the Crimean War. The distinguished artist William Powell Frith said of it: 'Never can I forget the impression that Leech's drawing made upon me!...Of all Leech's work, this seems to be the finest example....' It refers to Tsar Nicholas' boast in a speech during the winter of 1854/5 that 'Russia has two generals in whom she can confide – Generals Janvier and Février' (a *ukase* is an edict of the Tsar). He had hoped that the bad weather would put paid to the Allies' hopes in the same way that it had to Napoleon's 40 years earlier. Unfortunately for Russia things turned out differently this time.

'General Février' Turned Traitor
John Leech, *Punch*, 10 March 1855

The Young Czar Coming Into His Property
John Leech, *Punch*, 17 March 1855

The Black Choker
Dedicated to the Powers That Be
Private Jones: 'Here! Hi! Bill!! C-c-c-c-catch hold o' my musket!
My head's c-c-c-coming off!'
John Leech, *Punch*, 3 June 1854

The Real Use of the Bear-Skin Cap – A Hint to the Guards
John Leech, *Punch*, 25 February 1854

Highland Officer in the Crimea, according to the Romantic
Ideas of Sentimental Young Ladies.

Ditto, according to the Actual Fact.

John Leech, *Punch*, 12 January 1856

'Well, Jack! Here's good news from home. We're to have a medal.'
'That's very kind. Maybe one of these days we'll have a coat to stick it on?'
John Leech, *Punch*, 17 February 1855

There were many complaints by British soldiers that their clothing and equipment was inadequate for the conditions in the Crimea. In a letter to Thomas Delane, editor of *The Times*, the war correspondent W.H.Russell, commenting on the poor conditions of the British hospitals in comparison to the French ones, said: 'While these things go on, Sir George Brown [the first British general to arrive in the Crimea] only seems anxious about the men being clean-shaved, their necks well stiffened and waist belts tight. He insists on officers and men being in full rig; no loose coats, jackets etc.' The continued use of stiff leather neck stocks was a particular cause of irritation and the bitter winter of 1854/5 was felt badly by the British who had inadequate winter clothing and shelter. In addition a hurricane blew away many of their tents and sank two supply ships laden with ammunition and winter clothing. Amongst the improvised clothing devised by the troops to keep out the cold was the Balaklava helmet, a close-fitting knitted woollen hood that covered all of the head except the face. Other kinds of outfit that had their origin in the Crimean War were the cardigan (a collarless woollen sweater buttoned down the front, named after the sort worn by Lord Cardigan) and the raglan overcoat (named after Lord Raglan), which had sleeves extending to the neck without a shoulder seam (also later a type of pullover made the same way).

The decoration referred to in the Leech cartoon on this page is the Crimean Medal. However, on 29 January 1856, after the conflict was over, Queen Victoria endorsed the Duke of Newcastle's idea to create a new classless award for conspicuous bravery along the lines of the French Légion D'Honneur. Known as the Victoria Cross, the medal was a Cross Patté with a crown surmounted by a lion and the words 'For Valour' and was originally made from the metal of bronze cannon captured from the Russians at Sebastopol. Queen Victoria made the first 62 presentations of the award at a ceremony held in Hyde Park on 26 June 1857.

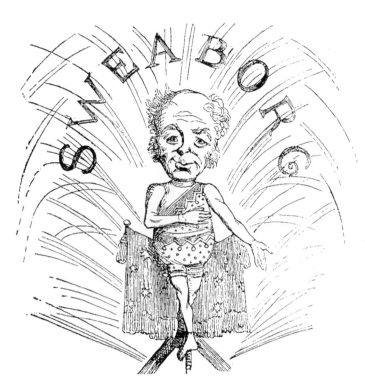

Palmerston's Blaze of Triumph
John Leech, *Punch*, 25 August 1855

The Return from the Baltic!!
British Lion: 'Oh yes, I'll come back – but I must just leave
a card at Cronstadt first!!!'
John Leech, *Punch*, 23 September 1854

Though most of the war was conducted on the Crimean Peninsula in the Ukraine, there were also a number of engagements in the Baltic Sea. The Royal Navy blockaded and bombarded Russia's main Baltic fortified naval base at Kronstadt on Kotlin Island in the Gulf of Finland, 14 miles west of St Petersburg, in September 1854. (Here they encountered the first ever use of floating mines at sea.) And in the Battle of Sveaborg (9-11 August 1855) a British fleet under Admiral Richard Dundas bombarded the Russian fortress at Sveaborg (now Suomenlinna), 'the Gibraltar of the north', in the harbour of Helsinki, Finland. They also used new shallow-draft ships armoured with two 68-pound guns and known as 'gunboats' which were able to get in close to the Russian defences. (Highly successful after the war in other regional conflicts of the British Empire they gave rise to the expression 'gunboat diplomacy'.)

Though it was left in ruins Sveaborg was not captured by the British. However, shortly afterwards, following an eight-day siege by the British Baltic Fleet under Admiral Sir Charles Napier and an invasion by 10,000 French troops under Marshal Achille Baraguay d'Hilliers (commander of the French force in the Baltic), the Russian fort of Bomarsund in the Gulf of Bothnia fell to the Allies on 16 August 1855. The Russian governor and 2400 troops were taken prisoner and the fort was destroyed. The first ever Victoria Cross for a naval exploit was awarded during this action when Mate Charles Lucas picked up a live shell that landed on the deck of HMS *Hecla* and threw it overboard (he later became a rear admiral).

In the first drawing by John Leech (*above left*) the British lion, dressed in a Royal Navy admiral's uniform, is seen going to Kronstadt, while in the second Lord Palmerston walks a tightrope as fireworks go off spelling out the name Sweaborg.

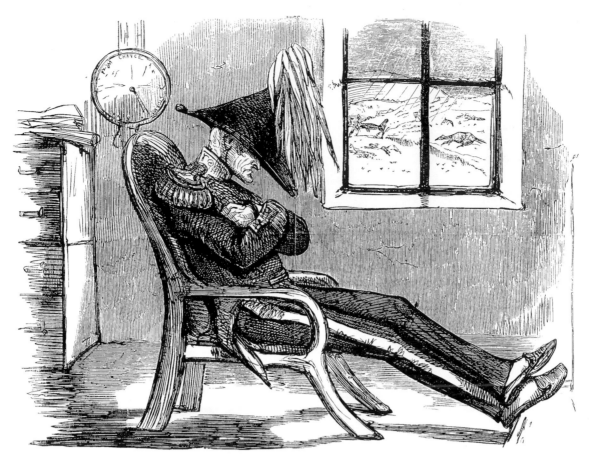

The General Fast (Asleep). Humiliating – Very!
John Leech, *Punch*, 24 March 1855

Queen Victoria was very concerned for the welfare of British troops in the Crimea. In the lower drawing (*right*), dressed as Britannia, she offers her sword to a Christian altar. The second cartoon (*above*) alludes to her Royal Proclamation that 21 March 1855 should be set aside as a national 'Day of Solemn Fast, Humiliation and Prayer' to ask for Divine blessing on British soldiers and the early restoration of peace in the Crimea. Lord Raglan, commander-in-chief of British forces in the Crimea, was heavily criticised for his inactivity. (Note the stretcher-bearers carrying wounded and the dead horses in the snowscape seen through the window and the fact that the barometer points to 'Stormy'.)

Lord Raglan (Fitzroy James Henry Somerset, 1st Baron Raglan), the 8th son of the Duke of Beaufort, had been an aide on Wellington's staff in the Peninsular War and later was his military secretary (losing his sword arm in the Battle of Waterloo in 1815). He succeeded Wellington as commander-in-chief in 1852 and, though he had never held an active command, led the British Army in Crimea. As W.H.Russell of *The Times* wrote to a friend: 'He is a good brave soldier, I am sure, and a polished gentleman, but he is no more fit than I am to cope with any leader of strategic skill.' Ten days after the defeat of the British at the Redan (see p.37) he died of dysentery on 28 June 1855, less than a year after he had been made field marshal (after the Battle of Inkermann). He was succeeded as commander-in-chief of British Forces in the Crimea by Major-General Sir James Simpson.

England's War Vigil
John Leech, *Punch*, 6 May 1854

The Harvest of the War
John Leech, *Punch*, 22 September 1855

Kladderadatsch (Berlin), 1855

At the 2nd Battle of Balaklava on 22 March 1855, the Russian Army besieged in Sebastopol made another sortie and lost 2000 men. On 24 May an allied amphibious operation captured the important Russian supply port of Kertch (commanding the entrance to the Sea of Azov), 150 miles from Balaklava. On 17-18 June, after a three-day bombardment, Allied forces launched a major attack on the Redan (a V-shaped defencework) and the Malakoff (the main fort) of the Sebastopol fortifications but failed though lack of further artillery support, losing 2184 killed and wounded. Then, at the Battle of Chernaya on 16 August 1855, the Russians made a final unsuccessful attempt to break out. Three divisions under Gorchakov made a sortie to the east at Chernaya where they met 35,000 French and Sardinian troops. The Russians lost 8000 men and 260 officers, while the Allies lost 1700.

Then a French force succeeded in taking the Malakoff on 8 September 1855. The French commander, General Aimable Péllissier, had noted that the Russians changed their guard at exactly the same time every day and thus with split-second timing caught the sentries unaware – this was the first time in history that an attack had been made at a pre-specified moment by officers using synchronised watches (for this Péllissier was later made a marshal). The French success made the Russians scuttle their fleet, blow up their magazines and abandon the city and though the Russian Army had not been defeated this effectively ended the war.

The news of the fall of Sebastopol – 'the eye-tooth of the bear' – in September was greeted with great rejoicing by the troops as can be seen in the Leech cartoon (*opposite, top*). The German drawing from *Kladderadatsch* (*opposite, bottom*) shows Britain and France dividing up the spoils of Sebastopol with the British lion offering Sardinia a bone while Turkey begs for scraps. The French cartoons by Gustave Doré have French soldiers laughing as Tsar Alexander II tries to scare them with a jack-in-the-box labelled '1812' – the date of Napoleon's retreat from Moscow and the destruction of his Grand Army – and then shows them stuffing the date down the Tsar's throat.

The Devil for Small Children
Gustave Doré in *La Sainte Russie* (1855)

'Now we'd like to stuff your big mouth!'
Gustave Doré in *La Sainte Russie* (1855)

All But Trapped
John Leech, *Punch*, 3 November 1855

On 16 June a Russian Army of 25,000 attacked and then laid siege to the fortified Turkish town of Kars – the former capital of Armenia in the Caucasus in northeastern Turkey – held by British Major-General William Fenwick Williams. The Allied forces were eventually defeated on 29 November when supplies ran out. The besieging Russian commander General Mikhail Muravyov in accepting the surrender said to Williams: 'You have made yourself a name in history and posterity will stand amazed at the endurance, the courage, and the discipline which this siege has called forth in this remnant of an army.'

On 21 November 1855 Sweden formed an alliance with France and Britain and joined the other Allies in the war against Russia. In 'All But Trapped' the Russian bear is surrounded by soldiers from (left to right) Turkey, Sardinia, Britain and France, indicating that the war is nearly over.

The British Lion Smells a Rat
John Tenniel, *Punch*, 15 March 1856

On 16 January 1856, though the Russian Army had not been defeated, Tsar Alexander II accepted the proposals put forward by neutral Austria and the Crimean War officially ended. On 1 February 1856 peace negotiations began. On 19 February, the Ottoman Sultan, Abdul Mejid, issued a reform edict guaranteeing his Christian subjects security of life and property and the right to exercise freedom of conscience. In March the Peace Conference opened in Paris under the Presidency of the French Foreign Minister, Count Alexandre Walewsky, and despite initial suspicions by Britain (*see above*), was a success.

Peace
Punch, 3 May 1856

On 30 March 1856, Britain, France, Russia, the Ottoman Empire, Piedmont-Sardinia, Austria and Prussia signed the Treaty of Paris. Amongst the clauses in the treaty was the demilitarisation of the Black Sea (including the demolition of Sebastopol and three other Russian naval bases and the withdrawal of the Russian fleet from the area). There were fireworks and huge peace celebrations in London and elsewhere. In February 1857 British and French naval forces ended their occupation of the Greek port of Piraeus and in March the Austrian Army evacuated Moldavia and Wallachia.

THE INDIAN MUTINY

THE INDIAN MUTINY of 1857-58 was a bloody wake-up call for the British Empire. Coming soon after the Crimean War against Russia the Sepoy Rebellion, as it was also known (or, in India, the First War of Independence), exposed the cracks that eventually led to the loss of India ('the Jewel in the Crown') and the break-up of the Empire itself a century later. It began as a minor revolt in Meerut near Delhi in northern India and led to a much wider conflict in which Indian troops ran amok, killing British women and children as well as soldiers. The mutineers later took Delhi, the old imperial capital, and restored its aged king as the new Mogul Emperor. They also captured Lucknow and in a particularly gruesome episode slaughtered more than 200 women and children in the British garrison at Cawnpore and threw their mutilated bodies down a dry well.

At first the British garrisons, which had been greatly reduced due to troop withdrawals for the Crimea, could barely contain the situation. None the less, order was eventually restored by British reinforcements helped by the majority of Indian troops who had remained loyal to the Crown. However, so incensed were the British commanders by the treatment of civilians, especially at Cawnpore, that there was a widespread call for vengeance. As a result many atrocities were also committed on the British side – including tying mutineers to cannon and blowing them apart. Eventually Lord Canning, the new Governor-General of India, managed to calm both the British public at home and the troops in India and peace was restored. The King of Delhi was exiled to Burma and the British East India Company was disbanded. In its place came direct British rule of India by a Viceroy who in turn reported to a new Secretary of State for India in London.

The Indian Mutiny – The Animal Trainer John Bull in Need
'Caran D'Ache' (Emmanuel Poiré), *Figaro* (Paris), 1857

In the mid-19th century British India was divided into three presidencies – Bengal, Bombay and Madras – each with its own governor, bureaucracy, army and commander-in-chief and under the general control of the British East India Company (whose headquarters, East India House, were based in Leadenhall Street, London). Each of the armies had British officers and the native Indian private soldiers were called *sepoys* in the infantry and *sowars* in the cavalry. On 10 May 1857 three regiments of infantry in the (mostly Muslim) Bengal Army stationed at Meerut (now Mirath, Uttar Pradesh) mutinied, shot and killed their officers, released military prisoners and in all some 2000 troops marched on the capital, Delhi, 40 miles to the southwest. The reason for the mutiny was the introduction of new cartridges for the French-designed Minié rifle (in service in an Enfield version with the British Army since the Crimean War) which were covered with greased paper which had to be torn open with the teeth. The grease used was a mixture of pig fat (abhorrent to Muslims) and cow fat (abhorrent to Hindus). The revolt was also supported by some Indian princes. Of the 74 regiments of infantry in the Bengal Army, 45 mutinied and 24 others were disbanded. In the Bombay presidency only two regiments were affected and in the Madras presidency none.

The two *Punch* cartoons shown here blame the insurrection on the mismanagement of India by the British East India Company. In a speech to the House of Commons in July 1857 Conservative Party leader Benjamin Disraeli – shown here (*top right*) in the guise of an Indian sepoy brewing up a stew with 'King Oudh sauce' – denounced the British Liberal government's Indian policy (which had recently been extended to make English the official language and to abolish the historic practices of *suttee* [widow-burning], infanticide and thuggism) and suggested that an official commission should be sent to India to hear the grievances of the King of Oudh and the mutineers. Oudh (Awadh), which lay between Bengal and the Punjab, with its capital at Lucknow, had been an independent kingdom but had recently been annexed by the British Governor-General, Lord Dalhousie, in 1856. It had also supplied 40,000 sepoys – nearly a third of the entire Bengal Army – and, as a result of the resentment the annexation caused, its Hindu soldiers formed a hard core of the Mutiny.

In the other Leech cartoon (*right*), Mr Punch, dressed as an Indian soldier, executes the East India Company by tying the victim to the front of a cannon (note the jester's hat to indicate the foolishness of the company).

The French cartoon (*opposite*) shows a number of hungry Indian tigers getting out of their cage to confront a fat John Bull caught off guard while eating his lunch.

The Asiatic Mystery, as Prepared by Sepoy Disraeli
John Leech, *Punch*, 8 August 1857

Execution of 'John Company' or, the Blowing Up (There Ought to Be) in Leadenhall Street
John Leech, *Punch*, 15 August 1857

Full Marching Order – The Penance of Panmure
John Leech, *Punch*, 22 August 1857

As the Delhi Siege continued other cities in northern India came under attack by the mutineers. Notable amongst these were the holy Islamic city of Allahabad and, notoriously, Cawnpore (Kanpur, on the Ganges, 245 miles southeast of Delhi), the East India Company's military headquarters in Oudh. On 4 June 1857, c.3000 sepoys of the Bengal Army garrison there mutinied and were joined by Nana Sahib (real name Dundhu Panth, the adopted son of the last Mogul ruler of India), the Maharaja of Bithur, who became their leader. The remaining 900 European troops under the command of General Sir Hugh Massy Wheeler – including many women and children – held out from a fortified position but after repeated bombardments and lack of supplies accepted Nana Sahib's terms of surrender. On 27 June the remaining 450 marched out of the city to the Ganges – about a mile from the city – where boats were supposed to take them to safety. However, they were massacred instead and the 200 survivors imprisoned. These, mostly women and children, were later themselves butchered and some were even thrown down a well.

Hearing of the massacre of the garrison at Cawnpore, General Sir Henry Havelock, in a remarkable forced march in the hottest season of the year, led 2500 British and Sikh troops 126 miles from the British port at Calcutta in nine days, defeating the forces of Nana Sahib at the Battle of Futtehpore (Fatehpur), 50 miles southeast of Cawnpore. He then confronted more forces led by Nana Sahib on 12 July in the Battle of Aong on 15 July before entering Cawnpore on 17 July where he discovered the mutilated bodies of European men, women and children. He exacted fierce revenge on any captured rebels, forcing them to clean up the blood and hanging them all. After awaiting reinforcements he then marched to Lucknow.

The first cartoon by John Tenniel (*opposite, top*), which was published over two pages in *Punch*, was immensely popular and made his reputation. It was suggested by Shirley Brooks (later editor of *Punch*) and such was its impact that the following week he reproduced it on the recruiting officer's flag in his cartoon 'Willing Hands for India' (another double-page cartoon) – shown below – and it later became a very popular print. In a review of some of Tenniel's book illustrations the following year the *Illustrated London News* said: 'Mr Tenniel's reputation stands too high to need eulogy, and the noble engraving which he supplied to *Punch* a few months ago, depicting the "British Lion's Vengeance", is in every household.' As *Punch* historian R.G.G.Price has said: 'the design has a tremendous melodramatic verve. The tiger is really tigerish, and the whole composition has the force of intense conviction, like some of the biblical subjects of the generation after Blake.' After Tenniel died *Punch* published a special 16-page supplement in his honour, written by its then editor, Owen Seaman. In it Seaman said that this drawing was 'one of the great English historic drawings' and 'the first cartoon in which the artist's great power displayed itself – on which his moral intensity was stamped'. He also praised Tenniel's depiction of the British lion throughout his career: 'No one, not Landseer himself, has so translated into line, stone or colour, the grandeur of the lion. Tenniel's lion was truly the king of beasts...a lion such as only an artist who was also a single-minded patriot of profound devotion could draw.' The Leech cartoon (*above*) refers to the fact that Lord Panmure (Secretary of State for War) refused to allow British troops in India to abandon their leather stocks and thick clothing even in the intense heat.

The Meerut mutineers, joined by the mutiny of the garrison in Delhi, reinstated the aged Mohammed Bahadur Shah – the last Mogul ruler of India and then living on a pension in Delhi – as the Emperor Bahadur Shah II and murdered every European in the city. A small band of British soldiers held out at the arsenal within the Red Fort for a short while and then blew it up. Many were killed in the explosion but miraculously Lieutenants Raynor and Forrest and Deputy Assistant Commissary John Buckley survived and after managing to escape were awarded the Victoria Cross (Raynor, aged 61 years and 10 months, remains to this day the oldest winner of the VC).

On 17 May 1857, 3000 British troops under General George Anson, commander-in-chief in India (and on his death from cholera by Major-General Sir Archdale Wilson), set off from Umballa (Ambala) 120 miles northwest of Delhi and arrived outside the city, then held by c.30,000 mutineers, on 8 June. After almost daily fighting there was a determined assault, preceded by a three-day artillery barrage, led by Brigadier-General John Nicholson on 14 September. Six days later the city fell. British losses of about 4000 included Nicholson himself who was shot in the chest on 14 September and died eight days later.

The British Lion's Vengeance on the Bengal Tiger
John Tenniel, *Punch*, 22 August 1857

Willing Hands for India
John Tenniel, *Punch*, 29 August 1857

The Siege of Lucknow, on the Gumti River in the province of Oudh, 270 miles southeast of Delhi, began on 1 July 1857 when the British Chief Commissioner, Henry Lawrence, together with nearly 500 women and children and a single regiment of troops, faced rebel forces at the British Residency in the city. After the death of Lawrence, Lieutenant Colonel John Inglis took command until Henry Havelock's troops fought their way to the city from Cawnpore. However, Havelock's troops were unable to raise the siege and were forced to join those trapped in the Residency. (Havelock later died during the siege and was seen as a national hero, immortalised in Tennyson's poems 'Havelock' [1858] and 'The Defence of Lucknow' [1879].)

The siege was eventually raised by Sir Colin Campbell. Appointed commander-in-chief of India on 11 July 1857 (following Anson's death from cholera in May) the 65-year-old hero of the Crimean War (commander of the 'Thin Red Line' at Balaklava) departed from England the next day, arriving in Calcutta on 13 August. After leaving a force at Cawnpore he set off for Lucknow on 9 November with 4700 British and Sikh troops. On 16 November 1857 he rescued the occupants and then, with the help of 10,000 troops supplied by the kingdom of Nepal, captured the heavily defended city itself on 21 March 1858. More than 3000 rebels were killed (thousands escaped) for the cost of some 700 killed and wounded on the British side. Amongst those involved in the battle were the first black man ever to win a Victoria Cross, Able Seaman William Hall, RN (who had

been born a British subject in Canada) and Lieutenant Roberts of the Bengal Artillery (later Earl Roberts of Kandahar who would achieve great fame during the Afghan and Boer Wars and who had been born in Cawnpore). A measure of the ferocity of the fighting during the relief of Lucknow is that on 18 November alone 24 Victoria Crosses were awarded – the highest ever total for a single day's combat. (There were 182 awards of the Victoria Cross during the Mutiny.) The First Battle of Cawnpore took place on 26 November when the garrison which Sir Colin Campbell had left en route to Lucknow was again attacked. Major-General Sir Charles Ash beat off 3000 troops of the Gwalior Contingent (the formidable and well-disciplined British-trained army of the state of Gwalior – one the five major Indian states – which had joined the rebels) under Tantia Topi (Ramchandra Panduroga) – responsible for the earlier Cawnpore massacre – but was eventually forced to retreat when rebel reinforcements arrived.

The Second Battle of Cawnpore took place on 6 December 1857 when Sir Colin Campbell returned from Lucknow with 5000 infantry, 600 cavalry and 35 guns and defeated 25,000 mutineers under Tantia Topi for the loss of only 99 men in what is seen by many as the turning point in the Indian Mutiny.

The dramatic cartoon by Tenniel (*opposite*) emphasises the outrage felt by the British public at the slaughter in Cawnpore and Lucknow and the revenge wreaked by Sir Colin Campbell on his arrival in India.

Every Inch a Soldier
Pam (Boots at the British Lion): 'Here's your hot water, sir.'
Sir Colin: 'All right. I've been ready a long time.'
John Leech, *Punch*, 25 July 1857

Justice
John Tenniel, *Punch*, 12 September 1857

In September 1857 General Wilson stormed and
took Delhi (taking Bahadur Shah prisoner) and
by the New Year Sir Colin Campbell could report
to the Prime Minister Lord Palmerston that most
of the major rebel cities were in British hands and
the Indian Mutiny was effectively over. However,
the new Governor-General of India, Lord Canning
– son of the former Tory Prime Minister, George
Canning – was seen by many as being far too
lenient on the rebellious sepoys. His proclamation,
issued after the suppression of the mutiny, was
universally condemned. (Charles, Earl Canning,
had replaced James Broun-Ramsay, 1st Marquess
of Dalhousie, as Governor-General of India in
1856.)

Too 'Civil' By Half
The Governor-General Defending the *Poor* Sepoy
John Leech, *Punch*, 24 October 1857

The Clemency of Canning
Governor-General: 'Well, then, they shan't blow him from nasty guns;
but he must promise to be a good little sepoy.'
John Leech, *Punch*, 24 October 1857

The New Year's Gift
Pam (to Sir Colin): 'Well – upon my word – eh! – I'm really extremely obliged
to you – but – eh! – how about keeping the brute?'
John Leech, *Punch*, 2 January 1858

The year 1858 was really one of mopping-up operations. Sir Hugh Rose with two brigades of the Bombay Army relieved the siege of the fort at Saugor, attacked and defeated the Rani of Jhansi on 3 April and the forces of Tantia Topi soon afterwards. On 1 March Sir Colin Campbell, with an army of 25,000, defeated mutineers in Oudh and Lucknow, and in the Battle of Gwalior on 19 June 1858 the Rani of Jhansi was killed.

On 31 August 1858, in an engagement with rebels at Seerporah, Captain Samuel Browne of the 46th Bengal Native Cavalry received a Victoria Cross for charging a nine-pounder gun to prevent it firing on infantry. Having cut down several of the gunners he was himself wounded in the left knee and a sword slash severed his left arm at the shoulder. As a result he invented the now famous Sam Browne leather belt – with a strap over the shoulder and a sword frog – and was later knighted.

The Accession of the Queen of India
John Leech, *Punch*, 11 September 1858

'New Crowns for Old Ones!' (Aladdin Adapted)
John Tenniel, *Punch*, 15 April 1876

Kaiser-i-Hind, 1877
Linley Sambourne, *Punch*, 13 January 1877

Lord Canning declared a 'State of Peace' throughout India and in August 1858 Parliament passed the India Act which transferred all the authority of the East India Company to the Crown and a new Cabinet post, Secretary of State for India, was created. Queen Victoria became Queen of India and the governor-general was replaced by a viceroy. Queen Victoria was later proclaimed Empress of India (*Kaiser-i-Hind* in Hindi and Urdu) at the suggestion of Prime Minister Benjamin Disraeli, who was himself elevated to the peerage as the Earl of Beaconsfield in 1876.

John Leech, *Punch*, Title Page, Vol. 35 (July-December 1858)

THE OPIUM WARS

THE OPIUM WARS with China began, like the Indian Mutiny, with the commercial interests of the British, who had been trading with Chinese ports since the 1790s. The First Opium War (1839-42), as it became known, started during the reign of the Manchu Emperor Tao Kuang (Hsuan Tsung), when the Chinese government attempted to prevent the illegal importation of opium and other narcotics from foreign merchants, notably the British Empire, then the world's largest producer of opium (by the 1830s opium accounted for 40% of the value of all Indian exports). Known as the 'devil drug', by 1888 it was estimated that 7 out of 10 Chinese men were users of opium. In March 1839 the Emperor appointed a special commissioner to the main trading port of Canton. He withdrew all Chinese labour from foreign warehouses, confiscated huge quantities of British-owned opium and ordered its destruction. Outraged, the British demanded compensation but when the Chinese government refused, Britain declared war.

The Second Opium War (1857-58) began as a result of a badly handled minor diplomatic incident in Canton while the Third Opium War (1859-60) was really an extension of the Second as its object was the enforced ratification by China of its peace treaty – the Treaty of Tientsin – supposedly agreed in 1858. Finally the suppression of the Boxer Rebellion (1900), the fourth war with China by Britain and its allies in 50 years, had as its object the defence of British and other European personnel (including Christian missionaries) who had been attacked and killed by patriotic Chinese rebel troops eager to expel all 'foreign devils' from their homeland.

The Presentation of the Chinese Ambassador
John Leech, *Punch*, 17 December 1842

John Leech, *Punch*, 21 March 1857

On 31 December 1838 the Chinese Manchu Emperor Tao Kuang (Hsuan Tsung), fed up with the trade in opium which was destroying the Chinese people and making vast profits for foreigners, appointed Lin Tse-hsu (Lin Zexu) as imperial commissioner to deal with the problem. As a result, the following year, Lin Tse-hsu confiscated 20,000 chests of British-owned opium in the southern Chinese seaport of Canton (Guangzhou) on the Pearl River – the main trading port with the West and capital of Kwangtung province – and proceeded to destroy it. When the Chinese government refused to pay compensation and also expelled the British community to the nearby island of Hong Kong, Britain declared war in June 1840 and sent 4000 British and Indian troops and 16 warships to the area. The first action of the war took place on 5 July 1840 when ships of the Royal Navy led by the 74-gun HMS *Wellesley* bombarded the port of Ting-hai (Dinghai) on Chu-san (Zhousan) Island close to the important coastal cities of Hangchow (capital of Chekiang province) and Shanghai.

In February 1841 the British under Commander-in-Chief General Sir Hugh Gough (who had been knighted in 1815 for service in the Napoleonic Wars), attacked the Bogue forts on the Pearl River defending Canton. In July 1841 Gough moved north and captured Chinkiang (Ching-keang Foo), 40 miles east of the ancient imperial capital of Nanking (China's second largest city). In August the British took the important port of Amoy and on 19 June 1842 they captured Shanghai. After the Royal Navy threatened to start a massive bombardment of Nanking from ships on the Yangze River the Chinese surrendered. The Treaty of Nanking – negotiated by Henry Pottinger (later [1843] the first governor of Hong Kong) – was signed on board HMS *Cornwallis* on 29 August 1842 in Nanking harbour. By this treaty, China was forced to cede the island of Hong Kong to Britain for 150 years and to grant trading concessions at five other ports – Nangpo, Foochow, Canton, Amoy and Shanghai – to British traders. China also had to pay a huge sum in compensation.

The cartoon by John Leech (*opposite*) was drawn after diplomatic relations with China had been restored. Printed only five months after *Punch* was founded it shows the new Chinese ambassador being presented to Queen Victoria by Prime Minister Robert Peel. It was the first ever international war-related political cartoon published in *Punch*. However, technically it should not be described as a cartoon at all, but rather as a 'big cut', as the word 'cartoon' in its modern sense did not come into use until the following year (on 25 July 1843) when Leech began his series of critiques of social injustices with his attack on the classical cartoon exhibition at Westminster with 'Cartoon No.1 – Substance and Shadow'.

The Great Chinese Warriors Dah-Bee and Cob-Den
John Leech, *Punch*, 7 March 1857

On the death of Emperor Tao Kuang (Hsuan Tsung), in 1850, his son Hsien Feng (Wen Tsung) ascended the throne and continued the anti-opium policy. On 8 October 1856 the British-registered lorcha *Arrow*, with an Irish captain and an all-Chinese crew, was seized by Chinese coastguards at the mouth of the Pearl River, Canton, on suspicion of smuggling opium. The Royal Ensign was removed and the 12 crew members were imprisoned. Though only carrying rice, not opium, it was owned by a Chinaman living in Hong Kong, had formerly been used for opium smuggling and three members of its crew were known pirates. Sir John Bowring, Governor of Hong Kong, demanded that the local viceroy, Yeh Mingchen, release the crew and when he refused Rear-Admiral Sir Michael Seymour (commander-in-chief of the China Station) shelled Canton in reprisal and destroyed the viceroy's palace. Earlier a French Roman Catholic missionary, Auguste Chapdelaine (who had entered the country illegally), had been beheaded by Chinese officials in Kwangsi. As a result of these two actions Britain and France jointly declared war on China on 3 March 1857.

Recoil of the Great Chinese Gun-Trick
John Leech, *Punch*, 11 April 1857

The shelling of Canton had the support of Prime Minister Lord Palmerston who had once said that 'such half-barbarian countries as China...need a dressing down every ten years or so'. However, it was condemned in the House of Commons by followers of Richard Cobden (a leading Radical) and in the House of Lords by the Earl of Derby (who said the *Arrow* incident was the 'most despicable cause of war that has ever occurred'). Gladstone, Disraeli, Russell – and even the Attorney-General Sir Richard Bethel – were also against it and a vote of no confidence brought about the immediate dissolution of Parliament and the fall of Palmerston. However, the British public were on Palmerston's side and he was re-elected in April 1857 to head a Liberal-Radical coalition government while, ironically Cobden lost his own seat.

Leech (*opposite, top*) has Palmerston dressed as a Royal Navy sailor facing Derby (with coronet) and Cobden dressed as Chinamen. Note the straw in Palmerston's mouth which from 1851 became a shorthand device used by cartoonists to identify him and originally referred to his fondness for horseracing. The 'Chinese gun-trick' (*opposite, bottom*) shows Cobden and his ally Bright dressed as Chinamen being knocked over by the recoil on their gun, illustrating the fact that both members for the Manchester area lost their seats in the subsequent General Election in April 1857.

Chinese resistance to the British attacks was fierce at first, as is suggested by the cartoons on this page. An edict from one Chinese governor declared: 'Let every inhabitant of China who shall meet an Englishman inflict on him the fate he merits...let everyone take part in the war, and teach foreigners to tremble before the will and before the anger of our Sovereign.' And posters stated: 'If we do not completely exterminate you pigs and dogs, we will not be manly Chinese.'

'What can you say for your friends now, Richard?'
John Leech, *Punch*, 9 May 1857

A Lesson to John Chinaman
Mr Punch: 'Give it him well, Pam, while you are about it!'
John Leech, *Punch*, 9 May 1857

Faced with superior firepower the Chinese were soon defeated, but when the Emperor refused to sign a treaty that would extend European trading rights in China a joint British and French force of 18,000 occupied Canton on 29 December 1857 and moved north. On 20 May 1858 Allied gunboats captured the five Taku (Dagu) forts that defended the mouth of the Peiho (Po Hai) River that led to Peking. They then proceeded upstream to Tientsin (Tianjin) – China's third-largest city – just 70 miles from the capital. At this point the 26-year-old Emperor Hsien Feng sued for peace. Negotiations between China, Russia, the USA and Britain (represented by Lord Elgin) produced the treaties of Tientsin signed in June-July 1858. This marked the end of the Second Opium War.

In 'A Little Tea Party' (*top left*) Britannia offers the Emperor of China Chinese black tea (known as 'gunpowder' tea) from a cannon-shaped teapot while Marianne of France looks on. (Note the willow-pattern design on the table, opium pipe on the floor and the shell-holes in the walls of the Chinese palace.)

A Little Tea Party
Britannia: '**A little more gunpowder, Mr China?**'
China: '**O-no-tan-ke-Mum.**'
John Leech, *Punch*, 4 September 1858

John Leech, *Punch*, 2 October 1858

The New Alliance
Emperor Louis Napoleon to Mr Bull: '**Is it not lucky, my dearest friend, that we have both been getting our guns into such good order?**'
John Leech, *Punch*, 24 September 1859

In June 1859 China abrogated its treaties of Tientsin and refused to allow French and British legations to Peking. The Third Opium War (1859-60) thus began when a British force under Rear-Admiral James Hope (who had replaced Admiral Seymour) once again bombarded the (by now rebuilt) Taku forts defending the river route to Tientsin and Peking on 25 June 1859. This time the Allies were defeated – three of the 10 gunboats were sunk and there were 500 casualties, including the admiral himself.

In 'The New Alliance' (*left*) Emperor Napoleon III in the guise of the French eagle in military uniform and John Bull as the British lion in hunting gear set off to attack the Chinese dragon while Mr Punch and his dog Toby look on.

In May 1860 an Anglo-French Force of 18,000 assembled in Hong Kong. In all there were 11,000 British and Indian troops under Lieutenant-General Sir James Hope Grant and 7000 French under General Charles Cousin-Montauban. On 26 July the joint force of 206 vessels sailed to the mouth of the Pehtang River to attack Tientsin and Peking. By 21 August 1860 they had taken the Taku forts and were soon marching on Tientsin where negotiations with the Chinese allowed them to progress to the walled city of Tang-chao, only 4 miles from Peking, to discuss an armistice. On 18 September Sir Harry Smith Parkes was sent to parlay with the Chinese but when he and his party were imprisoned the Allies again went on the offensive. On 21 September the French under Montauban defeated Chinese forces led by General Sang-kol-in-sen (known to the British as 'Sam Collinson') in a pitched battle at the Palichao Bridge on the Yang-Liang Canal which connected the Peiho River with Peking. As a result Emperor Hsien Feng fled 80 miles north to Cheng-te (Jehol), leaving his half-brother Prince Kung in charge. On 22 September Prince Kung sued for peace but the allies demanded the release of their prisoners first and began to bring up their heavy siege guns to attack Peking's formidable walls – 40 feet high and 60 feet thick.

Meanwhile, to the north of Peking, outside the walls, stood the famous Imperial Summer Palace (the Yuen-ming-Yuen) – 80 square miles of beautiful gardens and lakes containing 200 pavilions as well as the palace itself. One of the wonders of the world, the buildings also housed countless treasures. On 8 October the British arrived to find that the Emperor had gone and the French had already begun to loot the palace. As a result they joined in themselves (Queen Victoria was later given a Pekinese dog found in the palace which she jokingly named 'Lootie').

Outside the walls of Peking the Allies gave the Chinese till noon on 13 October to surrender. With only 10 minutes before the bombardment was due to start, the gates of Peking were opened and the British envoy to China, Lord Elgin, marched in with 500 men. James Bruce, 8th Earl of Elgin, was the son of the man who had brought the Parthenon Freize (the so-called 'Elgin Marbles') from Athens to the British Museum. Elgin negotiated the peace terms, which included ceding the Kowloon Peninsula opposite Hong Kong to the British for 99 years, the payment of an indemnity and the return of Sir Harry Smith Parkes and the other prisoners. However, when news of the treatment of Parkes and his party reached Elgin (only 19 of the 39 prisoners were returned alive) he ordered the Summer Palace to be burnt down in reprisal on 20 October 1860. Stunned by this act, on 24 October Prince Kung agreed to the terms of the Treaty of Peking and also finally ratified the 1858 Treaty of Tientsin. The war ended, the Allies withdrew from China except for a garrison left at Tientsin, which had been declared a free port. The Russians also gained a long stretch of China's northern coastline which included the site of the future port of Vladivostok.

New Elgin Marbles
Elgin to Emperor: 'Come, knuckle down! No cheating this time!'
John Leech, *Punch*, 24 November 1860

The diplomats come, as usual, when it is too late, and everything has long been soaked in blood
Borszem Janko, Hungarian cartoon, 1900

The Dragon Which They Thought Was Dead
Francis Carruthers Gould, *Westminster Gazette*, 5 July 1900

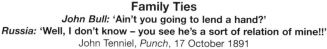

Family Ties
John Bull: 'Ain't you going to lend a hand?'
Russia: 'Well, I don't know – you see he's a sort of relation of mine!!'
John Tenniel, *Punch*, 17 October 1891

In the following decades there were a number of outrages against westerners in China. On the death of Emperor Hsien Feng in 1861 his widow, the Dowager Empress Tzu Hsi – who ruled as regent during the minority of their son, the boy Emperor Tung Chih (Mu Tsung) and continued as regent after his death during the reign of his successor, Kuang Hsu – had difficulty suppressing many rebellions against the Manchu dynasty. Notable amongst these was the Taiping (Great Peace) Christian revolt (1850-64) – probably the bloodiest civil war in the history of the world (between 20 and 40 million died). In March 1863 the British Major Charles Gordon (later to die at Khartoum) – who had taken part in the capture of Peking and the destruction of the Summer Palace in the Third Opium War and had remained in the country – earned the gratitude of the Chinese government (and the popular title 'Chinese Gordon') for leading the Chinese 'Ever Victorious Army' in attacks against the Taiping rebels in Shanghai, Nanking and elsewhere which contributed to their final defeat.

In May 1891 Chinese mobs destroyed Catholic and Protestant missions in the belief that they were kidnapping children. In December the same year an uprising against foreigners and foreign churches by the Golden Elixir Sect in Manchuria was eventually put down by the Chinese government. Britain, France, Germany and the USA united to protect their subjects in Manchuria but Russia remained aloof as it had links with the area after being granted a stretch of China's coastline that included Vladivostok (founded 1860) at the end of the Third Opium War.

The Boxer Rebellion began in May 1899 when 1500 foreigners and Chinese converts to Christianity were massacred by a group called the 'Society of Righteous and Harmonious Fists', which had started as a patriotic society devoted to martial arts, especially boxing. These Boxers, as they came to be known, quickly gained popular support with the tacit backing of the Dowager Empress Tzu Hsi who was against 'Western ideas'. Their actions included the burning of Christian churches and foreign embassies, and the destruction of the railway line between Peking and Tientsin. On 7 April 1900, British, US, German and French ministers sent a joint note to the Chinese government saying that they would land troops to protect their countrymen living in China if the Boxer rebellion was not suppressed within two months. On 31 May 1900 a small detachment (340 men) of British, US, Russian, Italian and Japanese marines arrived in Peking to help protect the foreign legations but soon found themselves under siege. As a result, on 10 June Vice-Admiral Sir Edward Seymour sailed for Peking with 2000 troops but was driven back. Then, after the murder of the German ambassador and more reports of the massacre of Europeans, a combined Allied force of 25,000 (including US, Japanese, Russian, British, Indian, French, Italian and Austrian troops) began to fight its way 80 miles inland from the coastal river port of Tientsin.

The Same Old Bear
Russian Bear (to British Lion): 'You've got so much to do elsewhere, I'll tackle this obstreperous party.'
British Lion: 'Oh thanks! But I wouldn't leave you alone with him for worlds!'
E.T.Reed, *Punch*, 13 June 1900

A Legacy of Discord
Chinaman: 'You allee chop-chop me now, but welly soon forrin devil chop-chop forrin devil!'
John Tenniel, *Punch*, 27 June 1900

The Avenger
John Tenniel, *Punch*, 25 July 1900

Europa to Chinese Emperor:
'If you can't put your foot down on him, I will!'
Hindi Punch, July 1900

In Reed's cartoon the British lion is still distrustful of the Russian Bear, even though Russia was an ally against China during the Boxer Rebellion. The other allies in the conflict appear to the right of the cartoon: the French poodle, the Japanese dragon and the German and American eagles. The allies appear again in 'A Legacy of Discord', a cartoon which proved prophetic. Fourteen years later the 'forrin devils' would indeed be attacking each other – in the First World War.

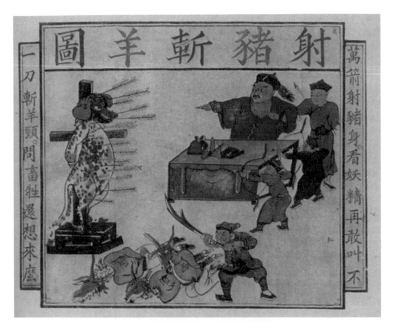

The Crucifixion of Christ
Chinese cartoon, c.1900

Chinese cartoon reproduced in *The Graphic*, August 1900

The Chinese Harvest
Borszem Janko, Hungarian cartoon, 1901

The Empress of China's Dream
Thomas Heine, *Simplicissimus* (Munich), 1900

The Allies continued to fight their way towards the capital against stiff resistance from the Boxers and on 14 August finally stormed Peking (by then defended by some 140,000 Boxers) to end the 56-day siege of the city. The Dowager Empress and the Emperor Kuang Hsu fled to Sian on 15 August 1900.

In the first Chinese cartoon (*top left*), commenting on the anti-Christian attacks of the rebels, Jesus is depicted as a pig being shot with arrows (*Jesus* means 'pig' in Chinese). The second Chinese drawing (*top right*) was reproduced in the *Graphic* from a Chinese newspaper and was in fact the first illustration of the fighting in Tientsin and Peking to reach Britain. It shows Europeans fleeing from the Boxers.

Li Hung Chang was known as the 'Bismarck of Asia'. He raised a regiment of militia to fight the Taiping rebels and, with the help of Gordon's 'Ever Victorious Army', captured Soochow and Nanking. He later helped negotiate the treaty with the Western powers that ended the Boxer Rebellion.

In the cartoon (*bottom left*) by Charles Harrison (fl.1883-d.1943) he is shown shocking the Imperial court with his Western dress, while Gould (*right*) puns on 'Eldorado' ('the golden one' in Spanish).

L Dorado.

> **L** is China s great big Li
> With his feather sticking high,
> You will also please to note
> Li's symbolic yellow coat.
> Here he tries to scorch away
> On a cycle through Cathay,
> While the Son of Heaven's Aunt
> Stamps her stump, and says he shan't.
>
> (12)

Francis Carruthers Gould in Harold Begbie, *The Struwwelpeter Alphabet* (1900)

Li Hung Chang
Charles Harrison, *Punch's Almanack for 1897* (1896)

The Empress Dowager of China
Charles Léandre, *Le Rire* (Paris),1900

THE ASHANTI WARS

THE ASHANTI WARS against the British took place on the Gold Coast (modern Ghana) on the northwest coast of Africa. The First Ashanti War began in 1824, in retaliation for a series of attacks on the peaceable Fanti coastal tribe by the slave-trading inland Ashanti, who were then the greatest power in West Africa. The British, who opposed the slave trade and had banned it in 1807, backed the Fanti. However, in a humiliating defeat, the Governor of Sierra Leone, Sir Charles MacCarthy, committed suicide after his British force was wiped out (his skull was later used as an Ashanti royal drinking cup), making Britain the first colonial power to suffer a major defeat by an indigenous African army. However, the British eventually prevailed and peace was agreed in 1831.

The Second Ashanti War followed forty years later, after Britain took over the forts on the Gold Coast evacuated by the Dutch in 1872 as agreed in a treaty the previous year. The Ashanti laid claim to one of the forts, Elmina, and were further incensed when the British offered protection to the Fanti, who denied the Ashanti access to the coast and a market for their slave trade. War began in 1873 when Major-General Sir Garnet Wolseley led a force of British troops into the area. He soon razed the Ashanti capital of Coomassie and deposed their king, Kofi Karikari.

In the Third Ashanti War the British again defended the coastal tribes against raids by forces under the new Ashanti ruler King Prempeh. A British invasion force under the command of Colonel Sir Francis Scott attacked in December 1895 and in less than a month had defeated Prempeh. A Fourth Ashanti War took place in 1900 after the British Governor of the Gold Coast, on a state visit to Coomassie, enraged the Ashantis by demanding to use their greatly revered Golden Stool as his own ceremonial seat. Besieged in the British garrison by thousands of angry warriors he managed to escape and a relief force eventually defeated the Ashanti in September 1900.

Fun, Preface to Vol. 18 (July-December 1873)

The Second Ashanti War was the first war in Africa to be widely covered by British press cartoonists and caricaturists as *Punch* had not begun until 1841 with *Fun* following in 1861 and *Vanity Fair* in 1869. These two illustrations to the Preface to Volume 18 of *Fun* show Mr Fun (*Fun* magazine's equivalent of Mr Punch) attacking Ashanti Warriors with his pen (*top*) while in the lower picture Major-General Sir Garnet Wolseley (leader of the British force) fires a cannon at them.

The British Lion Aroused
British Lion: '**Don't bully me, sir! I don't mind being kicked by one of my own size, but I'm not going to stand it from a little nigger like you!'**
Gordon Thomson, *Fun*, 4 October 1873

In June 1872 the Ashanti overran the Fanti tribe and attacked the British-held trading-post and fort of Elmina (which they laid claim to), but failed to capture it. In consequence, Wolseley was sent out from England in September 1872 to protect British interests. In January 1873 his force of 2500 troops entered Ashantiland. He soon razed the capital Coomassie (Kumasi), deposed their king,

Kofi Karikari (called King Coffee by British soldiers) and signed a peace treaty.

This cartoon is by Gordon Thomson (1840-c.1893) – *Fun*'s main political cartoonist for more than 20 years (1870-93) – and shows the British lion confronting King Kofi Karikari of the Ashanti (note the coffee pot on his head).

Sir Garnet Wolseley (1833-1913) was one of the best known British generals of Victorian times and was the inspiration for 'the very model of a modern major-general' in Gilbert and Sullivan's operetta *The Pirates of Penzance* (1880). He had served with distinction in the Crimean War (losing the sight of one eye at Sebastopol), the Indian Mutiny and the Opium Wars and became a household name during the Second Ashanti War when the phrase 'all Sir Garnet' became a synonym for efficiency. Also during the war he selected for his staff what became known as 'the Ashanti Ring' of hand-picked talented young officers, all of whom went on to become celebrated generals in their own right. These included Lieutenant-Colonels John McNeill and Evelyn Wood, Majors George Colley and Robert Home, and Captains Redvers Buller and Henry Brackenbury. The youngest general in the British Army, Wolseley later (1895) succeeded George, Duke of Cambridge (a cousin of Queen Victoria) as its commander-in-chief.

The large caricature of Wolseley shown here (*left*) is from *Vanity Fair*'s 'Men of the Day' series. The later drawing by Linley Sambourne in *Punch* (*below*) has him in the guise of a gamecock sporting tail feathers which show his battle honours ('Red River' refers to the first rebellion of Louis Riel against British rule in western Canada in 1869-70). The Thomson drawing (*right*) is the title page to Volume 18 of *Fun* and shows Wolseley about to stamp out the Ashanti leader (a coffee plant) with his huge boots as the Fanti (note the fans on their heads) look on and sing merrily. (Note also that the title has been changed to 'Funtee'.)

The Man Who Won't Stop
'Ape' (Carlo Pellegrini), *Vanity Fair*, 18 April 1874

Our Only General
Linley Sambourne, *Punch*, 1882

Gordon Thomson, *Fun*, Title Page, Vol. 18 (July-December 1873)

(*Opposite, top*) In a similar allusion to the effects of the singing and banjo playing of US-style 'Nigger Minstrels', the *Fun* artist suggests that the bagpipes of the 42nd Highland Regiment will simply frighten the Ashanti away.

(*Opposite, bottom*) In the triumphant parade 'Return from Ashanti' by Wallis Mackay (c.1850-1907) – note the smiling drum in the top row – Sir Garnet Wolseley appears mounted on a horse in the centre.

Our Allies
As they get on so badly with rifles, we would suggest that they be armed with something more suitable. With the dreadful costume and weapons depicted above, and issuing volumes of popular nigger melodies, they would do immense execution.
Gordon Thomson, *Fun*, 3 January 1874

The British evidently had little faith in their Fanti allies in the war against the Ashanti, as is shown in these two cartoons (note General Wolseley conducting the minstrels in 'Our Allies').

Our Allies Again!
'Yah, yah! White man come to help us. Golly, we help ourselves, yah!'
Gordon Thomson, *Fun*, 17 January 1874

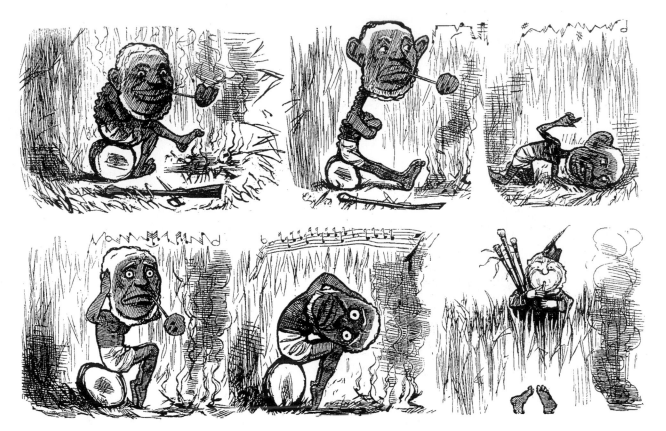

The Ashantee Sentinel – A Tale of the 42nd Highlanders on the Gold Coast
Fun, 10 January 1874

The Return from Ashanti
Wallis Mackay, *Fun*, 4 April 1874

'Were He a Worse Man, He Would Be a Better Statesman'
'Ape' (Carlo Pellegrini), *Vanity Fair*, 6 February 1869

Paradise and the Peri
' "Joy, joy for ever! My task is done – The gates are passed, and Heaven is won!" – *Lalla Rookh*'
John Tenniel, *Punch*, 28 February 1874

At the beginning of the Second Ashanti War, Britain's prime minister was the Liberal William Gladstone. However, in the General Election of February 1874 he was defeated and the Conservative leader, Benjamin Disraeli, became premier for the second time.

The allusion in Tenniel's drawing (*above*) is to the book *Lallah Rookh* (1817) by Thomas Moore, a hugely successful collection of four oriental tales in verse (which appeared in a new edition with illustrations by Tenniel in 1861). In one of these tales, 'Paradise and the Peri', a *peri* (a child of a fallen angel) is promised admission to paradise if she will bring the gift that is most dear to Heaven. After a number of false starts this proves to be a tear from a repentant criminal.

At the end of the Second Ashanti War, Sir Garnet Wolseley presented King Kofi's state umbrella to Queen Victoria. Note the helmets of the British 42nd and 23rd Regiments and the kneeling King Kofi in the *Punch* cartoon (*right*). Wolseley was later himself created a Baron and Viscount as is indicated in the *Fun* drawing (*below*).

Dearly Bought
Sir Garnet: 'It don't look much, Madam, but it has cost good money, and better lives.'
Britannia: 'And but for you, Sir Garnet, might have cost more of both!'
['King Coffee's Umbrella has been brought to England' – *Morning Paper*]
John Tenniel, *Punch*, 21 March 1874

A Fair Exchange
Her Majesty: 'Much obliged for the umbrella, Sir Garnet. Let me cap it with a hat!'
Gordon Thomson, *Fun*, 4 April 1874

Ashanti Again!
Britannia (to L-rd W-ls-l-y, 'the man who has been there'):
'You know all about the business, Commander-in-Chief.
But this time I expect something more than an umbrella.'
John Tenniel, *Punch*, 23 November 1895

After King Kofi was deposed by the British a civil war raged in Ashanti and King Agyman Prempeh (Kwaku Dua III) emerged as ruler. His defiance of the treaties agreed with the British led to the short Third Ashanti War. A British invasion force under the command of Colonel Sir Francis Scott attacked on 27 December 1895 and by 20 January 1896 had defeated Prempeh in an almost entirely bloodless campaign (though Prince Henry of Battenburg died a victim of the unhealthy climate). This expedition was the last time British troops went to battle in red tunics.

A Fourth Ashanti War took place in 1900 after Sir Frederick Hodgson, Governor of the Gold Coast, paid a state visit to the Ashanti capital, Coomassie, in March. When he arrived he demanded the submission of the Golden Stool of the Ashantis – a wooden seat greatly revered by the tribe – to use as his own ceremonial seat. The stool should have been surrendered to the British at the end of the Third Ashanti War but had been hidden away. The demand for its return led to anger by the tribe and Hodgson and his party were attacked by 40,000 enraged Ashantis who laid siege to the British garrison in Coomassie. On 23 June Hodgson and 600 native troops fought their way back to the coast. A punitive expedition by the West African Frontier Force, under Colonel James Willcocks, and the Gold Coast Constabulary – armed with machine-guns – was then sent to relieve the British forces left behind. In very difficult weather conditions at the height of the rainy season Willcocks and his force defeated the Ashanti at two major battles (14/15 September), relieved the garrison at Coomassie, and finally beat the Ashanti Army at Aboasu (Obassa) on 30 September 1900.

In the Reed cartoon (*right*) which appeared in *Punch*'s regular Parliamentary report feature, the reference is to the Irish MPs William Redmond (left), who thought the Third Ashanti War 'iniquitous' and John Dillon, who condemned it as 'inglorious and degrading'. Regarding the Fourth Ashanti War, there were very few cartoons of this as the British public were more preoccupied with the Boer War at that time.

The Ordeal of King Prempeh
'What's the charge, Sergeant?'
'Drunk and incapable, sir.'
'How do you know he's drunk?'
'He can't pronounce British interests, sir.'
[The king is still drunk. It seems that he was in mortal dread as to what would happen to him when he met Sir Francis Scott, and fortified his nerves accordingly in the orthodox Ashantee fashion
Central News telegram from Coomassie, January 21]
Francis Carruthers Gould, *Westminster Gazette*, 25 January 1896

Evicted from A-shanty!
King Prempeh: 'J'lly nice f'lers Re'mond an' Dill'n t' shtan' up fer a f'ler when he can' shtan' up fer 'imself! We won' go 'ome till mor- (hic).' *(And they didn't! House rose at 5.15am!)*
E.T.Reed, *Punch*, 21 March 1896

THE ZULU WAR

COMING SO SOON after a relatively easy victory in the Second Ashanti War, the Zulu War gave the complacent British Army a serious shock when it became evident that native African troops, armed only with spears and shields, could inflict a major defeat on a modern European military force. The conflict came about after friction began between King Cetewayo of Zululand in the southeast of South Africa and its neighbouring coastal state, the British colony of Natal.

Natal had become a British colony in 1842 and the region was peaceful until Cetewayo emerged as the victor in the Zulu Civil War of 1856 and began to threaten those who had escaped his regime into Natal. When Cetewayo refused to concede to British demands to dismantle his army, the local British commander Lieutenant-General Frederic Thesiger (shortly afterwards Lord Chelmsford) led a force of British and native Natal troops across the frontier in January 1879. After a humiliating defeat at the Battle of Isandhlwana the British made a heroic stand at Rorke's Drift on the Buffalo River and managed to beat off the Zulus before retreating back to the border. Before Lord Wolseley could arrive from England to replace him after this disaster, Chelmsford then invaded again (with heavy reinforcements) in March and eventually beat the Zulus at the Battle of Ulundi in July and in August captured Cetewayo himself. Zululand was annexed into Natal in 1897.

An Awful Example
There was a most cheeky Zulu; Shere Ali cried, 'Mind what you do.
I have tried the same game, to my infinite shame,
And you will get *sat upon* too.' [*Nursery Rhymes for Little Niggers*]
Gordon Thomson, *Fun*, 5 February 1879

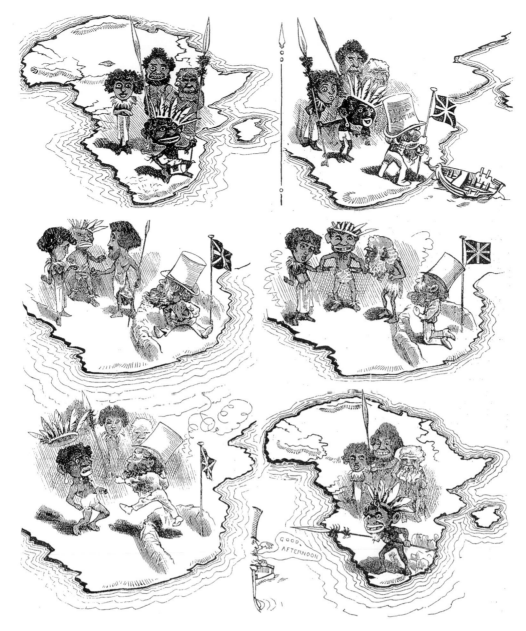

**An Epitome, of certain little affairs south of the Equator;
with the climax as fondly hoped for by the black gentlemen – *which it won't***
Fun, 12 May 1879

Zululand shared a 100-mile border with Natal. After Cetewayo became king in 1856 he built up an army of 50,000 men, most equipped only with shields, spears and clubs. To Sir Henry Bartle Frere, Governor of Cape Colony and High Commissioner for South Africa, Cetewayo was seen as 'an ignorant and bloodthirsty despot' who threatened the peace of the area and in December 1878 presented him with an ultimatum to disband his army and to fulfil a number of other demands, including ending what was seen as the oppression of his people (he killed thousands of his enemies after defeating his half-brother in the civil war of 1856).

When Cetewayo rejected Britain's ultimatum Lieutenant-General Frederic Thesiger (now Lord Chelmsford) invaded Zululand from Natal on 11 January 1879 with 16,800 troops (of which 6000 were British and 7000 were Natal Kaffirs) armed with rifles and bayonets plus a number of field guns. He had split his force into three columns and led the central column himself. Heading for Cetewayo's capital at Ulundi, 75 miles from the border, Chelmsford led his column across the Buffalo River at Rorke's Drift.

Thomson's cartoon from *Fun* (*left*) – drawn before news of the British invasion reached London – points out that the Zulu War

began at a time when Sher Ali Khan, ruler of Afghanistan, was also defying the British on the northwest frontier of India (see Afghan Wars, pp.82-91). Thomson draws Sher Ali standing on a torn-up British ultimatum which has led to his severe injuries and warns Cetewayo, with a new British ultimatum at his feet, not to make the same mistake.

In the second drawing from *Fun* (*above*) the cartoonist points out that another of the reasons for the British invasion of Zululand was because of Cetewayo's recent edict concerning the Zulu practice whereby men could only marry after they had served in the army. Cetewayo had decreed that two regiments of middle-aged warriors could marry a particular group of much younger wives. Unfortunately, most of these women were already betrothed. So when Cetewayo ordered that any of them found living with a man under 40 years of age would be executed and have her father's cattle confiscated many fled to Natal or the Transvaal (a number were executed). In the cartoon, 'Civilisation' is driven off by Cetewayo (wearing a headdress) after trying to stop an old man's marriage to a young girl.

71

A Lesson
John Tenniel, *Punch*, 1 March 1879

On the Track of the Zulu
Gordon Thomson, *Fun*, 19 February 1879

A Vote of Thanks
Field-Marshal Punch: Lieutenants Chard and Bromhead,
in the name of your country I thank you and all the defenders of Rorke's Drift.
You have saved not only a colony, but the credit of old England!!'
John Tenniel, *Punch*, 22 March 1879

By mid January Chelmsford had made a base at Isandhlwana hill, 10 miles from the border and 28 miles east of Dundee, Natal, but failed to fortify his camp. He then left half his column behind to go on a reconnaissance and it was then that the Zulus attacked. In the Battle of Isandhlwana on 22 January 1879 1000 African and 1800 British (including six companies of the 2nd Battalion of the 24th Regiment) were attacked by a Zulu *impi* (army) of 20,000. The defenders held out until they ran out of ammunition. No prisoners were taken and all but 55 British and 300 Africans were slaughtered – 1500 died. Chelmsford admitted 'We have been seriously underrating the power of the Zulu Army.' One of the survivors of the battle was Lieutenant Smith-Dorrien, later to become a distinguished general who served at the Battle of Mons in 1914.

The defeat at Isandhlwana – and the loss of an entire battalion – was a major blow to British morale. As these cartoons show, John Bull learnt a hard lesson, and Britannia and the British lion sought revenge (note the helmet and satchel of the 24th Regiment in the Thomson drawing).

The Battle of Rorke's Drift took place on 22-23 January 1879 in a mission station near a drift (ford) on the Buffalo River, a few miles from Isandhlwana and 25 miles southeast of Dundee in Natal. It was attacked by a Zulu *impi* led by Dabulamanzi, a half-brother of Cetewayo. After surviving for 12 hours before the Zulus retired exhausted, 11 men received the Victoria Cross, the largest number ever awarded for a single action. The commanders at Rorke's Drift were Lieutenants Chard and Bromhead who, with 120 men (including 36 wounded) of the 24th Regiment, defended the position against a force of 4000 Zulus. The British lost 17 killed while the Zulus' losses were about 400.

But just look at the difficulties some Generals have to contend with
Why, there's a General we know—(most intelligent fellow)—

Who only marched his troops straight on for a week, without any food—(to be sure, the Department had forgotten to issue boots to them; but that was a mere trifle)—and the fellows were positively unable to fight for fatigue, and got beaten! What can a General do with such troops as *that?*

Then the officers: Why, that General left one officer alone with *written orders* to keep back the enemy—and he actually let himself be killed by them!

Then the enemy's ways were so underhanded. Why, they came upon him *without any warning* when he was having a quiet cigar, and not even thinking of them! No General could deal with enemies like that!

The Difficulties of Some Generals!
Fun, 19 March 1879

Lord Chelmsford and Sir Henry Bartle Frere (Governor of Cape Colony and High Commissioner for South Africa) were much criticised for the humiliating defeat at Isandhlwana and Lord Wolseley was sent out from England to take command. Meanwhile, Prime Minister Disraeli (a weeping Mrs Dizzy in Thomson's cartoon, opposite) agreed that reinforcements should be supplied. Colonel Pullein – whose memorial Chelmsford, also weeping, is standing on – was the officer left in charge of the British camp at Isandhlwana in Chelmsford's absence. (Note the picture of the laughing Zulu on the wall.)

The Quill-driver
What we ought and what we ought not, to send out to Zululand, according to that very knowing and ubiquitous bird whose wisdom cries so loud just now from the newspaper columns, if not on the house-tops.
Linley Sambourne, *Punch*, 1 March 1879

The Mother's Pet
Mrs Dizzy: 'Did he get himself into a nasty mess? And did they say unpleasant things about him?
Never mind, my dear, here are some more soldiers to play with.'
Gordon Thomson, *Fun*, 19 March 1879

In Memoriam
'Home they brought her warrior, dead' – *Tennyson*
Gordon Thomson, *Fun*, 9 July 1879

During the Zulu War, the Prince Imperial, Eugene Louis Jean Joseph Napoleon – only son of Emperor Napoleon III and Empress Eugénie of France and thus heir to the French throne, who had been educated at the Royal Military Academy at Woolwich – had induced the British military authorities to let him join the British Army in Zululand. Unfortunately, despite senior British officers' attempts to keep him out of harm's way, he was killed on 2 June 1879 aged 23 while on a routine patrol in what was thought to be a safe area. On his death Disraeli observed: 'A remarkable people, the Zulus: They defeat our generals, they convert our bishops; they have settled the fate of a great European dynasty.'

The reference to Tennyson in Thomson's cartoon is to his poem *The Princess* (1847) which formed the basis for W.S.Gilbert's play of the same name (1870) and Gilbert & Sullivan's satirical opera *Princess Ida* (1884):

Home they brought her warrior dead.
She nor swoon'd, not utter'd cry:
All her maidens, watching said,
'She must weep or she will die.'

Polite Warfare
Cetewayo: 'So sorry about Isandlana; quite an accident, I assure you.'
Lord Chelmsford: 'Don't mention it, I beg. You must forgive me also for this little accident. I trust I am not putting you to inconvenience by penetrating into your interior.'
Gordon Thomson, *Fun*, 30 April 1879

**The Double Perambulator –
And the Nurse for our South African Babies**
Gordon Thomson, *Fun*, 11 June 1879

The Last Shy – Will He Do It?
Gordon Thomson, *Fun*, 18 June 1879

Despite further attacks by large numbers of Zulus, the British forces managed to survive using concentrated firepower. At the Battle of Kambula (29 March 1879) a force of 1900 European and African troops led by Colonel (later Field Marshal) Evelyn Wood (who had won the Victoria Cross in the Indian Mutiny) held off about 20,000 Zulus. And at the Battle of Ginginlov (2 April 1879) on the River Inyezanc (British soldiers called it 'Gin, gin, I love ya') a British column under Lord Chelmsford defeated a much larger Zulu force, killing 700 for the loss of some 48 British wounded and 13 dead. Note the bayonet stuck in Cetewayo's stomach (*above left*), a reference to his victory speech after the Battle of Isandhlwana when he said: 'An assegai has been thrust into the belly of the nation.'

The situation in Zululand was hotly debated in Britain. Despite the successes at Kambula and elsewhere it was still not believed that the war could be won until Lord Wolseley (pushing Frere and Chelmsford in the double pram) arrived in South Africa. In 'The Last Shy' (*left*) Disraeli is seen trying to knock down Cetewayo while Britannia, John Bull and the British working man look on.

Bravo, Chelmsford!
Cetawayo: 'Oh, Chelmy, Chelmy!
I didn't expect this of you.'
Gordon Thomson, *Fun*, 30 July 1879

Cleaning His Boots
'So far as I am concerned, the war is over' – *Lord
Chelmsford, after the victory of Ulundi*
Gordon Thomson, *Fun*, 6 August 1879

The End of the Zulu War
John Bull to his Captive: 'Well, you've shown
yourself a plucky little chap; but how could you
expect to punch my head?'
Gordon Thomson, *Fun,* 19 May 1879

Who is it grumbles at Income Tax ?
I point with pride to the slaughtered blacks !
Talk of squandered money and wasted lives—
Think what yards of crape are wanted by their widowed wives !
And loudly cheer, with three times three,
The pretty little coronet, and great big *B* !

British postcard, c.1880.

Lord Chelmsford's forces eventually reached Cetewayo's capital at Ulundi, 115 miles northeast of Durban, and the Battle of Ulundi took place on 4 July 1879. The British were hugely outnumbered – 5317 infantry and 899 cavalry with 12 field guns and two Gatling guns faced 20,000 Zulus – but none the less the battle lasted only 30 minutes with c.1500 Zulu dead for the loss of 15 British killed and 78 wounded. Cetewayo escaped but was later caught by Wolseley. The success at Ulundi greatly improved Chelmsford's standing in Britain as can be seen in the second cartoon (*top right*) in which none other than the Prime Minister, Benjamin Disraeli, is cleaning his boots. (Note Chelmsford's battle-stained uniform and helmet.) The reference to the Turnerelli wreath concerns a 'people's tribute' to Disraeli for his achievement of 'Peace With Honour' at the 1878 Berlin Congress on the subject of the so-called 'Eastern Question' regarding territorial claims in the Balkans and Asia Minor. Unfortunately, Disraeli refused the gold laurel wreath, designed by the leading artist Edward Turnerelli, and thus Thomson suggests that Chelmsford should have it.

In the postcard (*bottom right*) the figure reading the paper, the 'great big B!' responsible for the loss of life in Zululand, is again Disraeli (by now Lord Beaconsfield).

After being captured by the British in September 1879, Cetewayo was exiled to Cape Town but in 1882 he was brought to England where he met Queen Victoria at Osborne House (she described him in her journal as 'tall, immensely broad and stout, with a good-humoured countenance and an intelligent face'). However, once arrived, there was some confusion about what should happen to him. In the *Punch* cartoon (*top left*) it is suggested that he be exhibited by The Great Farini, who organised events at the Royal Aquarium in Westminster. This was a large building opposite Westminster Abbey which opened in 1876 and was demolished in 1906 to make way for the Methodist Central Hall. As well as containing a huge water tank for performing aquatic feats it also acted as a sort of music hall and put on various popular entertainments and freak shows. Farini had been exhibiting Zulu warriors there since 1879. (Born William Leonard Hunt, in New York, Farini was a retired high-wire walker who in his youth had been a rival of the more famous Blondin.)

On 29 January 1883 Cetewayo was allowed to return to Zululand but after civil war broke out he died on 8 February 1884. Zululand itself was annexed by Natal in 1897.

A Black 'White Elephant'
John Bull (puzzled): 'He's cost me enough to catch him! And now I've got him what am I to do with him?'
The Great F-rini (with alacrity): 'Might I suggest the Aquarium?'
John Tenniel, *Punch*, 27 September 1879

Cetawayo's Coming!
What'll they do with him?
'No reasonable offer refused!'
Linley Sambourne, *Punch*, 8 July 1882

The Restoration of King Cetewayo, or 'Tidings of Comfort and Joy'
Gordon Thomson, *Fun*, 23 August 1882

Restored
'Spy' (Leslie Ward), *Vanity Fair*, 26 August 1882

Vulcan Arming Neptune
John Leech, *Punch*, 19 April 1862

The 'British Tar' of the Future
John Leech, *Punch*, 12 April 1862

The 'Ugly Duckling'
Neptune: 'Well, of all the hideous–!'
Britannia: 'Ah, she isn't pretty, certainly; but remember,
Father Nep, handsome is that handsome does!'
John Tenniel, *Punch*, 3 May 1873

Bustling Him Up
Sir E.J.Reed: '**Come, Mr Goschen, this will never do. You're getting left behind in the matter of speed!**'
[In a letter to the *Times*, Sir Edward Reed, while approving in the main recent Admiralty designs, points out a lamentable lack of speed in recent cruisers for the British Navy as compared with those in Foreign Navies.]
E.T. Reed, *Punch*, 22 March 1899

At the start of the Crimean War in 1854 the Royal Navy had no iron warships, the bulk of its fleet comprising three-decker 'ship of the line' sailing ships with guns on each deck in the style of those used in the Napoleonic Wars. During the siege of Sebastopol the British fleet consisted of only two steam ships of the line, the rest were sailing ships moved into position by steam tugs. With the launch of the French ironclad frigate *La Gloire* in 1859 an arms race began and the first British armoured ship was HMS *Warrior* (1860). In 1863 Edward J. Reed (father of the cartoonist E.T.Reed) became Chief Constructor for the Navy. Reed had been impressed by the battle between the heavily armoured ships *Merrimac* and *Monitor* during the American Civil War in 1862 and began a new programme of shipbuilding. The first British ship with no masts, sails or rigging which relied entirely on steam power (and which had screw propellers instead of paddle wheels and turret-mounted guns) was HMS *Devastation* (1873). Thereafter the navy began to employ ever larger 'ironclads' until HMS *Dreadnought*, launched in 1906, set a new pattern for big-gun, heavily armoured battleships. However, the early ironclads were disliked by sailors who saw them as unstable and unseaworthy 'coffin boats', a view that was brought to public notice by the accidental sinking of the *Birkenhead* (1852, 432 drowned), *Captain* (1870, 463 drowned), *Vanguard* (September 1875) and the near sinking of the *Iron Duke* in November 1875. The scandal that followed led to legislation to improve conditions on the ships.

In Reed's *Punch* cartoon (*above*) his father criticises First Lord of the Admiralty George Goschen (right) over the speed of British cruisers. The Russian drawing (*right*), however, shows how much the Royal Navy's fleet of ironclads was feared worldwide as John Bull is turned into a huge, and massively armoured, aggressive sea serpent.

Neptune's Warning
Father Nep: '**Look here, My Lass. You used to "Rule the Waves";**
but if you *Mis-Rule* 'em, as you've done lately, by jingo there'll be a row!'
Britannia: '**I'm sure I don't know who's to blame, Papa dear!**'
Father Nep: '**Don't know!!! Then pipe all hands, and find out!!!**'
John Tenniel, *Punch*, 30 October 1875

S.F. Sokolowski, Russian cartoon, 1904

THE FIRST AFGHAN WAR (1839-42) started in April 1839 when a British Army under General Sir John Keane marched from northwest India into the walled city of Kandahar (Afghanistan's second largest city and erstwhile capital). The reason given for the invasion was that the Afghan leader, Emir Dost Mohammed Khan, was pro-Russian and Britain wanted to keep Afghanistan as a buffer state between British India and what was seen as an ever-expanding Russian Empire. Keane later overran the capital, Kabul, deposed the emir, and installed a new pro-British puppet ruler, Shah Shuja.

For a while all seemed calm and then in December 1841 the British envoy in Kabul was assassinated along with the entire British diplomatic mission. The British then agreed to leave and in January the following year 14,500 men, women and children departed with promises of safe passage to India. However, en route to the British frontier fort at Jalalabad, nearly all were massacred. The British retaliated with another invasion, via the Khyber Pass, and Dost Mohammed Khan was eventually restored to power.

After the emir's death in 1863 his third son, Sher Ali Khan, became Afghanistan's new ruler. In 1878 he in turn upset British sensibilities by accepting a Russian envoy but refusing a British one. This led to the Second Afghan War which began with another invasion of British and Indian troops. During the ensuing conflict Sher Ali Khan died and in 1879 his successor, his son Yakub Khan, sued for peace. However, within four months the new British envoy in Kabul was assassinated. Thus the British invaded again, this time under Lieutenant-General (later Lord) Frederick Roberts VC. Kabul was taken, Yakub Khan was captured and exiled to India, a peace treaty was signed and Abdur Rahman (a grandson of Dost Mohammed Khan) took the throne in July 1880. However, the same month almost 1000 British troops were killed at Maiwand near Kandahar by rebel troops loyal to Yakub's brother Ayub Khan. The remains of the British force fell back to the city of Kandahar itself and soon found themselves under heavy siege until General Roberts finally made a famous rapid march with 10,000 men from Kabul (280 miles in 20 days), defeated Ayub Khan and peace was restored.

Disturbed Dreamers
Salisbury: 'Wake up, wake up, my little men! – Don't make such a horrible noise! It's only the nightmare!!'
('It has generally been acknowledged to be madness to go to war for an idea, but it is yet
more unsatisfactory to go to war against a nightmare' – *Lord Salisbury among the Merchant Taylors*)
John Tenniel, *Punch*, 23 June 1877

In this cartoon by Tenniel the threat from Russia is seen as a nightmare (literally a ghost horse) ridden by a sabre-wielding Cossack as the British press (*Morning Post*, *Pall Mall Gazette* and *Daily Telegraph*) sleep. Watching over them all is Lord Salisbury, Disraeli's Secretary of State for India.

ASIATIC SPORT—SHERE STALKING.

Room enough !   Yes, no doubt, and abundance of game,
  Yet the two rival Sportsmen seem scarcely content.
Fine quarries'!   But what if both mark down the same ?
  The chance of collision 'twere hard to prevent.
Neutral ground ?   Very fine ; but if one cross the line,
  Though he swear with no notion of trying a shot,
To reprisal his rival will promptly incline,
  And suspect that his aim is to collar the lot.

This quarry seems shy ; but JOHN BULL has his eye
  On the Russian, who just reconnoitres, no more.
For suppose he *were* tempted a pot-shot to try,
  As J.B. recollects he was tempted before !
Room enough !   Ah ! why cannot these Sportsmen agree
  To take the Earl's tip, and steer clear of each other ?
If either try trespass, 'tis easy to see
  'Twill spoil sport, and result in no end of a bother.

Rival Sportsmen
'I say now, as I have said before, that there is room enough in Asia for both England and Russia' – *Lord Beaconsfield*
Linley Sambourne, *Punch*, 21 September 1878

The British were very suspicious of Russian influence on Sher Ali Khan, emir of Afghanistan, and in August 1878 – after Sher Ali had accepted a Russian envoy – sent General Sir Neville Chamberlain, then commanding the Madras Army, to Kabul to try and open diplomatic relations. This cartoon by Linley Sambourne uses a quotation from Prime Minister Disraeli (now the Earl of Beaconsfield) which tried to defuse the situation. It shows John Bull (in the guise of an Indian prince – note the Star of India in his turban made out of the Union Jack) – and Tsar Alexander II of Russia (who would be assassinated in 1881) as rival sportsmen stalking Sher Ali (depicted as an Afghan goat) either side of the Himalayas (the letters form the mountain range).

For a time Britain and France tried to restore order in Egypt which was in a very unsettled state under its Turkish rulers. In September 1881 the Egyptian Minister of War, Colonel Ahmed Arabi Pasha, led a military coup against Khedive Muhammad Tewfik Pasha in protest at French and British control of the Suez Canal and of Egypt's finances. He then began to fortify the important northern coastal port of Alexandria and when 50 Europeans were killed in riots in the city in June 1882 Admiral Sir Beauchamp Seymour sent Arabi an ultimatum to disarm or be bombarded. When Arabi refused to comply, a Royal Navy fleet shelled Alexandria 'in self-defence' in July 1882.

'Hold On!'
' "An allegory on the banks of the Nile" – *Mrs Malaprop*'
John Tenniel, *Punch*, 10 June 1882

Taming the Crocodile
Gordon Thomson, *Fun*, 26 July 1882

In Self-Defence
'We didn't want to fight, but by Jingo! when we did,
We had the ships, and had the men, who acted as was bid,
And batter'd Alexandria where Arabi was hid,
Against the orders from Constantinople.'
Gordon Thomson, *Fun*, 19 July 1882

In Tenniel's cartoon (*opposite, top*) for *Punch* John Bull, dressed as a sailor, and a French sailor grapple with the Egyptian crocodile. (Mrs Malaprop from Sheridan's play *The Rivals* [1775] mistakenly alludes to alligators on the Nile.) Gordon Thomson's cartoon (*opposite, bottom*) makes a similar point with the Khedive on the animal's back (note the insincere, 'crocodile tears') which is about to be shot by Prime Minister Gladstone carrying a battle drum (while a shocked John Bull, Kaiser Wilhelm of Germany and the goddess Isis – representing Egypt – look on). Thomson's second drawing (*above*) has John Bull (wearing the cap badge of HMS *Britannia*) between the British lion and British bulldog as

shells explode overhead. The verse is adapted from a popular music-hall song by G.W.Hunt from the time of the Russo-Turkish War when Disraeli sent the Royal Navy to Constantinople to protect it from Russia. The original verse (which gave rise to the word 'jingoism' for aggressive patriotism) was:

We don't want to fight, but by Jingo if we do,
We've got the ships, we've got the men, and got
  the money too.
We've fought the Bear before, and while we're
  Britons true
The Russians shall not have Constantinople.

The New Rifle – A Little More Military Muddling
HRH Commander-in-Chief: **'Look here, Tommy Atkins,
I've got another rifle for you; and if you're a good boy, and don't get killed,
perhaps some day we may think about giving you a proper one.'**
Gordon Thomson, *Fun*, 27 October 1886

There was considerable criticism of the ordnance and weaponry available to the British Army and Royal Navy in the 1880s. The single-shot, breechloading 0.45 calibre Martini-Henry Mark II rifle was still standard issue – the bolt-action 0.303 Lee-Metford with an eight-shot magazine was not introduced until 1888 and the more efficient 10-round 0.303 Lee-Enfield did not come into service till 1895. However, a major scandal followed when it was discovered that defective weapons were being supplied to the forces. A Government committee reported that a combination of official negligence and corruptness on the part of the contractors meant that the services were supplied with 'swords that bend, bayonets that twist, guns that explode, and cartridges that jam'.

Note that in Thomson's cartoon (*left*) Tommy Atkins is equipped with 'Real Jam Cartridges' and a corkscrew-shaped bayonet while Tenniel's vultures (*below left*) hovering over the dead soldier surrounded by bent swords and bayonets are labelled 'War Office' and 'Contractor'. Proof that such shoddy workmanship was still being supplied to the British Army a decade later is shown in the German cartoon (many foreign artists liked to draw the British as Scotsmen to ridicule their kilts).

Das englische Schwert

(Zeichnung von Th. Th. Heine)

The Vultures
John Tenniel, *Punch*, 23 April 1887

The English Sword
**'Oh if only it said "Made in Germany" then it
would be a lot better use!'**
Thomas Heine, *Simplicissimus* (Munich), 1899

Despite the inadequacies of their other arms the most significant new weapon introduced to the British Army at this time was the 0.45 calibre Maxim machine-gun which replaced the more cumbersome crank-operated Gatling gun. It was invented by the American Hiram Maxim (1840-1916) who emigrated to England and set up the Maxim Gun Company in 1884. Water-cooled, it was capable of firing 500 rounds a minute and was first used in action by the British Army in 1893. Maxims were used with devastating effect in the Battle of Omdurman in the Sudan in 1898 and also in the Boer War the following year. In the French cartoon by Amaral (*below*) the woman firing the gun in the Transvaal during the Boer War is none other than Queen Victoria herself.

One of the 'Maxims' of Civilisation!
Old and New
'Think of the glorious Mottoes,' said a Major of the old school.
'"*Nil Desperandum*", "Death or Victory", "England Expects" and so forth.'
Replied his friend the modern Captain, 'Bother your Mottoes!
Give us the "Maxims"!'
E.T.Reed, *Punch*, 2 December 1893

LA DAME DE CHEZ *MAXIM*. — par AMARAL

« Au Transvaal, les canons Maxim ont fait merveille. »

The Woman with the Maxim
'In the Transvaal the Maxim gun is a marvel.'
Carlo do Amaral, *La Caricature* (Paris), 30 December 1899

The Quarrelsome Graces
Nebelspalter (Zurich), 5 November 1898

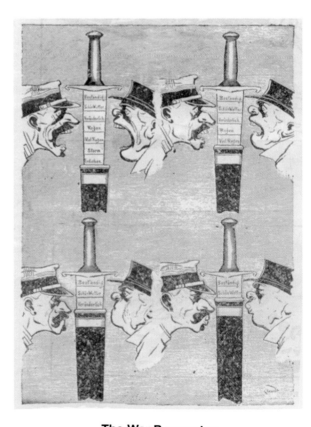

The War Barometer
Fashoda!!!, Fashoda!!, Fashoda!, Fashoda
Gustav Brandt, *Kladderadatsch* (Berlin), 30 October 1898

Airy Alf and Bouncing Billy take Fashoda
Ralph Hodgson, *Big Budget*, 15 October 1898

After beating the Dervishes at Omdurman, General Kitchener's troops continued to push south down the Nile. In September they encountered a French fort at Fashoda (Kodok) which had been set up in July by the explorer Major Jean-Baptiste Marchand who had invaded the Sudan from Brazzaville in the French Congo. Kitchener demanded that they should withdraw, threatening the use of his gunboats, but the French refused. This led to heated diplomatic exchanges between London and Paris and the serious possibility of war between the two nations. However, the matter was eventually resolved and the French were escorted out of the Sudan. (Marchand later served as a Lieutenant-Colonel in Kruger's army against the British in the Boer War.)

The final confrontation between the Anglo-Egyptian forces and the Mahdists was at the Battle of Umm Dibaikarat (23 November 1899) when 3700 Anglo-Egyptian troops under Francis Wingate defeated 5000 Dervishes under Khalifa Abdullahi (who was himself killed in the battle).

In the German cartoon (*left*) the French and British shout at each other and the sword between them acts as a barometer which reads: Earthquake, Storm, Heavy Rain, Rain, Changeable, Settled and Good Weather. Progressively the mood changes and in the end only the last two weather conditions remain. In the French cartoon (*opposite*) Britain is dressed as the wolf pretending to be the kindly grandmother in the tale of *Little Red Riding Hood* with France as the eponymous heroine (carrying Fashoda) whose cake the wolf wants to eat.

Little Red Riding Hood
'Grandmother, what large teeth you have!'
'That is to eat your cake, my child!'
Le Petit Journal (Paris), 20 November 1898

THE BOER WAR

THE FIRST EUROPEAN PRESENCE at the most southerly point in Africa was when the Dutch East India Company established a settlement at the Cape of Good Hope in 1652. This became a French base after Revolutionary France occupied Holland at the end of the 18th century, and was subsequently attacked and occupied by Britain during the Napoleonic Wars. When peace returned Holland ceded the base to Britain and British immigrants began to move into the area, by then known as Cape Colony. In 1834 the abolition of slavery in the British Empire alienated the slave-owning Cape Dutch or Boers ('farmers') who moved north (the Great Trek) from Cape Colony into what would become the Orange Free State and Transvaal. Britain recognised the independence of these two states in the 1850s. However, on the discovery of the world's biggest diamond fields in Kimberley in the Orange Free State, the city was annexed to British-run Cape Colony in 1871 and in 1877 Transvaal – by then bankrupt and threatened by Zulus – was annexed as a British colony.

After the defeat of the Zulus in the Zulu War (1879), and the coming to power in Britain of the formerly pro-Boer Liberal Party under William Gladstone (1880), the Transvaal Boers hoped they would get their independence back. However, when they did not they refused to pay taxes and rose in revolt in the Transvaal War (also known as the First Boer War, 1880-81), defeating the British at the battles of Laing's Nek, Majuba Hill and elsewhere and gaining a large measure of self-government as a result of the Treaty of Pretoria (5 April 1881).

On the discovery of the world's biggest goldfield in Witwatersrand (White Waters Ridge) – a 6000ft ridge, 150 miles long – in the southern Transvaal in the mid-1880s a mass of British and foreign immigrants known as Uitlanders ('outsiders') began to settle in the Transvaal but were taxed heavily and not given any official status or voting rights by the Boers. In 1899 the Uitlanders appealed to Britain for help and 10,000 troops were sent out to reinforce the garrison in the neighbouring British state of Natal (annexed in 1843). Threatened, President Kruger of Transvaal gave the British an ultimatum to withdraw their forces. When they refused the Boer War (also known as the Second Boer War, 1899-1902) began with Boer invasions of the British states of Natal and Cape Colony. At first the British fared very badly and the Boers successfully besieged the cities of Mafeking, Ladysmith and Kimberley. However, eventually the Boers were defeated and in 1902 peace returned to South Africa.

The School of Musketry
Boer (to Field Marshal HRH the Commander-in-Chief): 'I say, Dook!
You don't happen to want a practical "Musketry Instructor", do you?'
John Tenniel, *Punch*, 7 May 1881

The Transvaal or First Boer War (known to the Boers as the First War of Independence) began on 16 December 1880 when Boer forces besieged British garrisons throughout Transvaal (an area almost twice the size of England and Wales) and proved themselves to be far better marksmen than their opponents, more mobile and better at camouflage. Without uniforms or pay, the Boers also provided their own horses and guns. At the Battle of Bronkhorstspruit (20 December 1880) British troops were ambushed at a village 38 miles east of Pretoria by 200 Boers and lost 155 killed and wounded (the Boers only lost 7).

Major-General Sir George Colley – British High Commissioner for South East Africa and commander-in-chief of British troops in Transvaal and the neighbouring British province of Natal – then organised a force to relieve the Transvaal garrisons and to suppress the uprising. However, when his force of 1000 troops dressed in white helmets and scarlet coats attacked from Newcastle he was defeated at the Battle of Laing's Nek (28 January 1881) – a pass in the Drakensberg mountains on the Transvaal/Natal border – by General Piet Joubert (Commandant-General of Boer forces).

On 8 February 1881 the British were defeated again at the Battle of Ingogo and later the same month at the disastrous Battle of Majuba Hill (modern Amajuba, the Hill of Doves, 6600 feet above sea-level) in northwest Natal, 75 miles north of Ladysmith. During the night of 26-27 February a British force of about 650 soldiers and sailors under General Colley climbed to the top of Majuba Hill which overlooked the large Boer camp of General Joubert. Feeling safe, the British were unprepared when the Boers attacked, with the result that Colley himself was killed and 223 British were killed or wounded and 50 were taken prisoner for almost no losses to the Boers. The British government were furious at the news of the defeat and Queen Victoria herself said: 'I do not like peace before we have retrieved our honour.' None the less the British sued for peace soon afterwards and the Treaty of Pretoria (5 April 1881) gave the Boers a large measure of self-government.

The cartoon by Tenniel (*opposite*) reflects the British mood at the time, which put the blame for the British military failure in the Transvaal on George, 2nd Duke of Cambridge, the Hanoverian-born grandson of George III (and thereby a cousin of Queen Victoria) who had been appointed commander-in-chief of the British Army in 1856 and held the office for nearly 40 years. A conservative opposed to army reform he was much criticised for the defeats at Majuba Hill and elsewhere which drew attention to the superiority of the marksmanship of the Boers. The cartoon featuring a tiny John Bull (*right*) shows British ambitions in southern Africa from the pro-Boer perspective (Kidger Tucker was himself from Johannesburg, Transvaal).

New Version of an Old Fable
A frog once thought himself as big as a bull – but he came to grief
William Boucher, *Judy*, 11 May 1881

'Which is the Paramount Power?'
Kidger Tucker, South African cartoon, c.1898

A Round in Favour of Kruger
John Bull: 'Ah well; I knew when I took him on
I should not have it all my own way!'
J.M.Staniforth, *Western Mail*, 12 December 1899

The Times are Out of Joint
''Tis unnatural,
Even like the deed that's done. On Friday last,
A falcon, tow'ring in her pride of place,
Was by a mousing owl hawk'd at and maimed.'
Macbeth, Act II, Scene IV
J.M.Staniforth, *Western Mail*, 19 December 1899

HONNI SOIT QUI MAL Y PENSE...!

Au seuil de la nouvelle année, M. Chamberlain présente son œuvre
à Sa Gracieuse Majesté.

Honni Soit Qui Mal y Pense...!
**On the threshold of the New Year, Mr Chamberlain
presents his work to her Gracious Majesty**
Jean d'Aurian, *Le Grelot* (Paris), 15 January 1900

The New Gulliver: 'Well damn it all!
I seem to have trod in a really disgusting anthill.'
French cartoon, 1900

The hopes raised by the arrival of Buller were short-lived. Though Lord Methuen defeated the Boers at the Battle of Belmont (23 November 1899) and the Battle of Modder River (28 November) en route to Kimberley, in the infamous 'Black Week' – beginning 10 December 1899 – the British lost the battles of Stormberg, Magersfontein and Colenso. At Stormberg (a railway junction 50 miles south of the Orange River in Cape Colony) on the 10th a British force of 3000 under General William Gatacre was defeated by Boers under Jan Olivier (the British lost 135 killed and nearly 700 captured). At Magersfontein on the 11th Lord Methuen was beaten by Boers under Piet Cronje (971 British casualties including the death of Major-General Andrew Wauchope).

Then on 15 December Buller himself was defeated at Colenso, a village on the Tugela River, 16 miles south of Ladysmith. Buller's force of 20,000 met an equal number of Boers under Louis Botha (who had taken over as Commandant-General of Boer forces after Joubert had resigned through ill health on 25 November). Buller lost 1100 men (including Lieutenant Frederick Roberts, the only son of Field Marshal Roberts, who won the first ever posthumous VC), while Boer casualties were negligible.

In the drawings by Staniforth (*opposite, top*), John Bull receives a black eye from Kruger (note his glove labelled 'Gatacre' has been removed) while Buller is Shakespeare's wounded falcon 'hawk'd at' by the owl Joubert. ('The time is out of joint' is actually from *Hamlet*, and the original *Macbeth* quotation has Tuesday, not Friday and 'kill'd' not 'maimed'.) In the first French cartoon (*opposite, bottom left*) Chamberlain – carrying a bag of dum dum bullets and with the title deeds to gold mines in his pocket – shows a horrified Queen Victoria a pile of British skulls topped by a wreath saying 'To our sons'. The second one (*opposite, bottom right*) has an aged and scrawny John Bull, dressed as the God of War (and carrying a bag of dum dum bullets), stepping into an anthill marked 'Transvaal' and being bitten by Boer 'insects'. By contrast is Tom Browne's up-beat comic strip (*above right*) from the cover of *Illustrated Chips*. Here his popular heroes, Weary Willy and Tired Tim, having beaten the Boers and taken Pretoria, welcome the arrival of Sir Redvers Buller.

The Noble Army of Weary Unwashed Wanderers Spifflicate the Boer Army
Tom Browne, *Illustrated Chips*, 23 December 1899

Hands Across the Sea (New Version)
New York World (New York), 8 September, 1899

John Tenniel, Title Page, *Punch,* Vol. 119
(January-July 1900)

Ein schöner Zug

A Beautiful Procession
The Prince of Wales performs his duty as Commander of the famous Dog Brigade at the
homecoming of his wounded countrymen
Gustav Brandt, *Kladderadatsch* (Berlin), 1899

When the news of 'Black Week' reached Britain there was a public outcry and disbelief that the British Army should be faring so badly against the Boers. Buller was now called 'Sir Reverse Buller' by his own troops and Queen Victoria herself (speaking to Balfour) said: 'We are not interested in the possibilities of defeat; they do not exist.' As a result the government despatched Field Marshal Lord Roberts and Lord Kitchener to South Africa on 23 December 1899. Reinforce-ments were also sent in the form of the newly created City Imperial Volunteers (CIV) as, unlike most major countries, there was no conscription in Britain at this time (it was not introduced until 1916). The 1500 members of the CIV were financed by the City of London (the Government only supplied weapons and ammunition) and drawn from London and the Home Counties. More than 30,000 volunteers also came from the Imperial Yeomanry and further help came from Britain's colonies, including 16,000 troops from Australia and c.6000 each from
New Zealand and Canada. (One notable Australian recruit was Harry 'Breaker' Morant, later the subject of a book and film.)

John Tenniel (*top left*) shows Mr Punch and his dog Toby leading reinforcements in the form of the City Imperial Volunteers. The German drawing 'A Beautiful Procession' (*top right*) refers to the fact that the main part of the Imperial

Under One Flag
Linley Sambourne, *Punch*, 18 October 1899

Ein armer notleidender Menschenfresser bittet um eine milde Gabe

**A Poor, Needy Maneater Begs
for a Charitable Gift**
Ernst Retemeyer, *Kladderadatsch* (Berlin), 1901

Yeomanry was the Royal Wiltshire Regiment, known since 1863 as the Prince of Wales's Own. It shows the future Edward VII in command of a pack of dogs to welcome wounded soldiers back to Britain.

A similar contrast is between the two cartoons on Empire recruits. Sambourne (*above left*) has the daughters of a strong Britannia – Canada and the various states of Australia – willingly drawing their swords to join the fight. The German cartoon (*above right*) has a different version of events, with an old, fat and broken down John Bull shown going cap in hand to Canada, India and Australia to collect just a few tiny and unhappy soldiers.

Lord Roberts of Kandahar sailed from Southampton on 23 December 1899, taking with him Lord Kitchener of Khartoum as his Chief of Staff. They arrived at Cape Town on 10 January 1900. Roberts (known familiarly as 'Bobs' and 'the pocket Wellington') was a small man and then 67 years old (a fact emphasised in the French portrait). None the less he was a greatly admired veteran of the Afghan Wars and much confidence was placed in him by the British. The German cartoon reproduced here (*top left*) takes the opposite view and shows a long chorus line of British generals defeated by the war in South Africa – the last being Buller – as Roberts struggles to make his cut in the Natal section of the world drawn as the apple of knowledge.

According to Leslie Ward, who drew the *Vanity Fair* print of Roberts (*top right*), 'This cartoon, on account of the subject, beat the record for popularity, and its sale exceeded that of all other cartoons in *Vanity Fair*.' Note that the mountain on the right shows the face of Kruger. Gould's cartoon (*bottom right*) refers to the 12 Labours of Hercules in classical mythology and shows Roberts as Hercules cleaning out the Augean stables whilst the skin of the slain boar (Boer) Kruger (the Boar of Mount Erymanthus) hangs on a hook and Britannia looks on.

The Fruit of Knowledge
Chorus of Africa-weary Generals:
'Ha! Will he really make the cut?'
Kladderadatsch (Berlin), 1900

'Bobs'
'Spy' (Leslie Ward), *Vanity Fair*,
21 June 1900

Lord Roberts – War is Money
Leal da Camara, *L'Assiette au Beurre* (Paris),
28 June 1902

Hercules
Francis Carruthers Gould in Harold Begbie,
Great Men (1901)

Too Hot to Hold
J.M.Staniforth, *Western Mail*, 27 January 1900

The British on Spion Kop
Caran D'Ache, French cartoon, 1900

Spion Kop
Kladderadatsch (Berlin), 1900

In the Battle of Spion Kop (19-24 January 1900), General Buller led 25,000 troops across the Tugela but was blocked by 8000 Boers under General Botha. None the less a detachment under Lieutenant-General Sir Charles Warren managed to seize the heights known as Spion Kop, 1470 feet above the River Tugela and 24 miles west of Ladysmith. Spion Kop ('Lookout Hill') was so named because it was here that the Boers' trekker forefathers had first sighted Natal. However, the Boers under Botha shelled the hill and soon reoccupied it, inflicting considerable losses on the British (1200 in a single day) who were forced back across the Tugela River yet again. Mahatma Gandhi was a stretcher-bearer at Spion Kop and this battlefield gives its name to Liverpool's football stands (known as The Kop) in memory of local regiments who lost men there.

The Tugela Problem
The Lion: 'Come out!'
The Oom Tortoise: 'Come on!'
Francis Carruthers Gould, *Westminster Gazette*, 8 January 1900

General Buller continued to make attempts to relieve Ladysmith by crossing the Tugela River but was constantly rebuffed by Kruger's forces under General Botha. At the Battle of Vaal Krantz (5-6 February 1900), his third attempt to relieve Ladysmith, Buller at the head of 20,000 men forced a crossing of the Tugela and seized the heights of Vaal Krantz southwest of the city. However, he was eventually repulsed yet again and retired behind the Tugela with losses of 374.

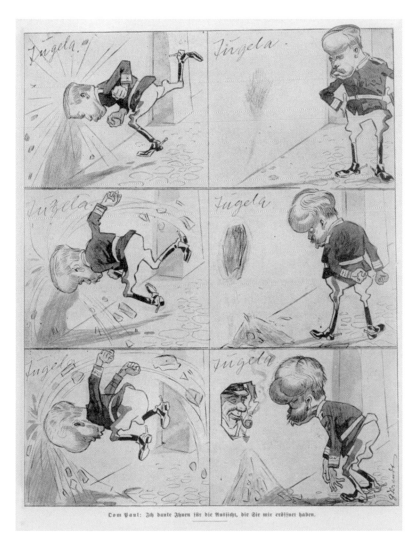

The Indefatigable
Oom Paul: 'Many thanks for the view that you have opened up for me.'
Kladderadatsch (Berlin), 1900

John Bull in South Africa
Johan Braakensiek, book cover (Amsterdam), 1900

'Bobs' to the Rescue
Cecil Rhodes: ' I knew you wouldn't fail, Roberts!'
J.M.Staniforth, *Western Mail*, 17 February 1900

The Napoleon of the Cape
Jean D'Aurian, *La Caricature* (Paris), 12 April 1902

Cecil Rhodes
Funeral Monument erected by Boer Subscription
Leal da Camara, *L'Assiette au Beurre* (Paris), 28 June 1902

CECIL RHODES.

Dem Protz sieht man es an | Er war ein fleiss'ger Mann
Er hat viel Geld und ob! | Und ist ein fauler Kopp.

Franz Jüttner, German postcard, c.1900

The first sign of recovery by the British under Lord Roberts was the relief of Kimberley by a cavalry force under General Sir John French (aided by Colonel, later Field Marshal, Douglas Haig) on 15 February 1900. For 133 days about 8000 Boers under Commandant Martinus Pretorius (and later General Piet Cronje) had besieged Kimberley, the centre of the diamond-mining operations in South Africa. The British garrison in the town numbered about 4000 men under Colonel Robert Kekewich and also present amongst the civilian population were Cecil Rhodes and fellow directors of De Beers. In fact it was Rhodes himself who had engineered the relief of the town. Lord Roberts had planned on attacking Bloemfontein and Pretoria to force the Boers to abandon their sieges of Ladysmith, Kimberley and Mafeking, but when Rhodes used his influence and threatened to surrender Kimberley to the Boers to stop the bombardment, the strategy was changed.

As can be seen in the French and German cartoons shown here, Rhodes was not well-liked in Europe and was blamed for the deaths of many British and Boer soldiers. 'The Napoleon of the Cape' (*opposite, top right*) was published shortly after he died in Cape Town in 1902 and shows the figure of death grabbing him as he sleeps on Cape diamonds and Boer gold while in the background Boer villages burn, women are beaten and civilians are hanged.

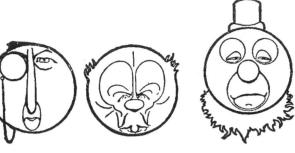

Geometrical Drawing
Chamberlain, Roberts, Oom Paul, Cecil Rhodes, Rudyard Kipling
Der Floh (Vienna), April 1901

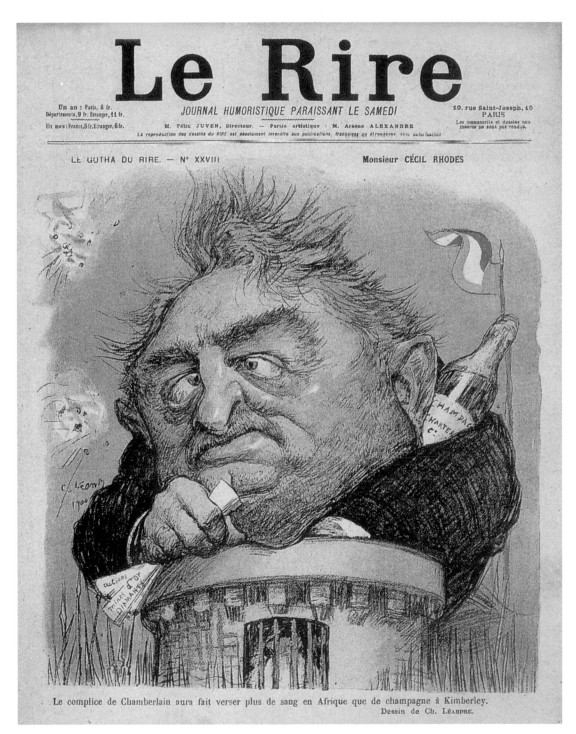

Cecil Rhodes
The accomplice of Chamberlain spilt more blood in Africa
than champagne in Kimberley
Charles Léandre, *Le Rire* (Paris), 17 February 1900

Such a Surprise
Mr Balfour: 'Fancy, Ridley! they've actually got horses!'
Sir M.W.Ridley: 'And look, Arthur, they've got rifles too. What a shame to deceive us!'
Francis Carruthers Gould, *Westminster Gazette*, 22 January 1900

As British troops faced repeated set-backs in South Africa questions began to be asked about the poor quality of the equipment that they had to use. It seemed that many in authority had totally underestimated not only the skill of the Boer troops but also the fact that they had better quality horses (especially remounts – replacements for those killed in action) and weapons supplied by France and Germany. These included modern German Mauser rifles as well as German and French field guns, including the 75mm Krupp (German) and 155mm Creusot (French) – known as the 'Long Tom' which outclassed all British cannon. (Their artillerymen were also German-trained and had German officers, and the Boers' volunteer International Brigade – led by the French Foreign Legion – included French, German, Dutch, Russian, Scandinavian and even Irish soldiers.) Much of this equipment – including ammunition and foreign reinforcements – was delivered to the Boers via the rail-link to Pretoria from the supposedly neutral port of Delagoa Bay (opened in 1895), the harbour of Lourenço Marques (now Maputo), capital of the neighbouring state of Portuguese East Africa (modern Mozambique).

In the cartoons shown here Arthur Balfour (the nephew of Prime Minister Lord Salisbury) was First Lord of the Treasury and Leader of the House of Commons (and later himself prime minister), Sir Matthew White Ridley was Home Secretary and the Secretary for War was Lord Lansdowne.

A Sort of Remount System
Some Expensive Studies in Anatomy (Dedicated to the War Office)
Francis Carruthers Gould, *Westminster Gazette*, 12 February 1902

A Question Within Range
Field Piece (to the Secretary for War):
'May it please your Lordship to say who is responsible for sending out little chaps like me to fight against great hulking fellows like that?'
G.R.Halkett, *Punch*, 3 January 1900

'The Queen! God Bless Her!'
Linley Sambourne, *Punch*, 29 November 1899

An Inconvenient Surprise
French postcard, 1900

British officers were frequently lampooned in the foreign press, especially in France. There was further opportunity for humour when Queen Victoria herself ordered 40,000 special decorated souvenir tins (each c.6 x 3$\frac{1}{2}$ inches) containing chocolate bars to be sent to the British troops at the front as her personal Christmas and New Year gift. Though much appreciated by the soldiers of the British Army it was much ridiculed by the foreign press at a time when the Boers seemed to be winning the war.

Storm and Sunshine
J.M.Staniforth, *Western Mail*, 19 February 1900

Owl (Cape Town), March 1900

'Bravo, Bobs!'
John Tenniel, *Punch*, 28 February 1900

The rapid advance of the British forces into the Orange Free State gave President Steyn pause for thought. The first major victory by the British in the field was at the Battle of Paardeberg (18-27 February). Here 5000 Boers (including their families) led by the Boer commander-in-chief, General Cronje, were surrounded at Paardeberg on the Modder River in the western Orange Free State, 23 miles south of Kimberley, by British troops under General (later Field Marshal) French. Lord Kitchener then took command but after sustaining more than 1000 casualties Lord Roberts himself took over and eventually forced Cronje to surrender on 27 February – the anniversary of the Majuba Hill defeat. Cronje was later imprisoned on the British island of St Helena in the South Atlantic (1100 miles off the west coast of Africa), as Napoleon had been after his final defeat at Waterloo in 1815. In all 24,000 captured Boers had been sent to British prison camps in St Helena, Bermuda, India and Ceylon by the end of the war.

Fortune of War
General Cronje (at St Helena, saluting the shade of Napoleon the Great):
'Same enemy, sire! Same result!'
Linley Sambourne, *Punch*, 14 March 1900

Ogden's Tobacco Advertisement, 1900

At Last!
Sir George White: 'I hoped to have met you before, Sir Redvers.'
Sir Redvers Buller, VC: 'Couldn't help it, General.
Had so many engagements!'
Linley Sambourne, *Punch*, 7 March 1900

The Ladysmith Number of the Big Budget, 24 February 1900

A Natural Phenomenon
It is strange, but true, that although it is winter time in the Orange Free State,
the Boers find it getting so warm for them that they are trekking north.
J.M.Staniforth, *Western Mail*, 18 April 1900

The Relief of Ladysmith was greeted with great joy in Britain. The British garrison in the town – 12,000 troops under the command of General Sir George White VC – had held out since 2 November 1899 until finally relieved by Buller with a force of 25,000 men on 28 February 1900. An officer in the South African Light Horse which relieved Ladysmith was Winston Churchill.

Bloemfontein, capital of the Orange Free State, fell without a struggle on 13 March. As President Steyn had already fled the city to make Kroonstadt his new capital, Lord Roberts marched in with 34,000 men, raised a Union Jack and annexed the state as the Orange River Province. General Joubert died on 27 March and a month later, on 25 April, British troops under Roberts relieved the Siege of Wepener, an Orange Free State town on the Caledon River, 63 miles southeast of Bloemfontein in which the British garrison of 1700 had been repeatedly shelled since 9 April by Boers under Christian De Wet (who had succeeded Cronje as Boer commander-in-chief). By the end of the month the southeast of the Orange Free State had been cleared by the British but the defeated Boers then fled north towards Transvaal. On 12 May Lord Roberts took Kroonstadt and President Steyn moved his capital to Heilbronn, itself captured on 22 May.

Whilst all the World Wondered
Our Neighbours: 'Mon Dieu; he, then, can get excited!
We never should it possible have thought!'
J.M.Staniforth, *Western Mail*, 22 May 1900

On 17 May 1900 the Siege of Mafeking was finally relieved. The enthusiasm in Britain was unparalleled – normally calm and disciplined Britons were ecstatic with joy and for 48 hours afterwards there were massive celebrations in London and throughout the Empire at the heroic stand that had been made by the British commander of the town, Colonel Robert Baden-Powell. Situated on the border between Transvaal and the British colony of Bechuanaland (Botswana) the Siege of Mafeking began on 13 October 1899 when Baden-Powell, with only 1251 men (mostly police), plus women and children, held off c.9000 troops under Piet Cronje. One of the most famous of Baden-Powell's dispatches during the siege was: 'All well, four hours' bombardment. One dog killed.' The siege lasted 217 days until the city was relieved on 17 May 1900 by Major-General Bryan Mahon. Such was the respect given to Baden-Powell's stand that he was promoted major-general aged only 43, the youngest ever, and the verb, 'to maffick' (meaning to celebrate extravagantly), entered the English language. (Baden-Powell later founded the Boy Scout movement.)

**Mafeking Night, or rather
3am the following morning**
Phil May, *Punch*, 1900

Mafeking
'Drawl' (Leslie Ward), *Vanity Fair*, 5 July 1900

Shifting His Capital
John Tenniel, *Punch*, 13 June 1900

John Bull's Triumph to Pretoria, 1900
Johan Braakensiek, *De Amsterdammer* (Amsterdam), 1900

Lord Roberts marched into the Transvaal and occupied Johannesburg on 31 May 1900. Seeing that the writing was on the wall, President Kruger abandoned his wife in the capital, Pretoria (which was overrun by the British on 5 June), moving to Waterval Boven and taking with him £2 million of State funds. Meanwhile, General De Wet had fought his way out of the Orange Free State and brought his troops 1000 miles to join General De la Rey northwest of Pretoria (harassing British convoys, garrisons and railways en route) and General Botha overpowered a British garrison at Nitrals Nek, 20 miles west of the capital.

In the Dutch cartoon (*above*) by Johan Braakensiek (1858-1940) John Bull is seen riding uncomfortably on Kruger who has been drawn as a porcupine. The implication is that Kruger's forces were still fighting a hard rearguard action against the British troops advancing from the Orange Free State's capital Bloemfontein to Transvaal's capital, Pretoria.

On 1 September Lord Roberts annexed the Transvaal and on 20 October Kruger – together with his £2 million of State funds – was taken on the Dutch man-of-war *Gelderland* to Lourenço Marques in neighbouring Mozambique and then on to Europe. Here he made speeches denouncing the barbaric practices of the British in South Africa – strenuously denied in Britain but finding much favour with French audiences. He eventually found refuge in Utrecht, Holland, where he was given the protection of Queen Wilhelmina of the Netherlands. Paul Kruger died in Clarens, Switzerland, on 14 July 1904 and was later buried in Pretoria.

In the French cartoon 'Vanquished...At Last!' (*below right*) John Bull (with a black eye) is shown rummaging through the pockets of Kruger's abandoned coat (note Bible and gold nuggets) while Boer farmsteads burn.

Jean D'Aurian, *La Caricature* (Paris), 17 November 1900

Dissolution!
The General Election will finally settle this business
William Duane, *Fun*, 25 September 1900

Vanquished...At Last!
Caran D'Ache, French cartoon, c.1900

143

Though not due until the following year, the Conservative government decided to hold a snap election while the country was still at war to take advantage of the public's buoyant mood. Thus in October 1900 Parliament was dissolved and a General Election was held. Known as the 'Khaki Election' (after the dust-brown cotton uniforms worn by British troops in the Boer War – *khak* is 'dust' in Urdu), the main issue was the war. The result was that the Conservatives increased their majority by four seats and thereby felt that they had a mandate to continue the war.

Political Slimness – A Khaki Issue
Lord S.: 'Get under cover – don't expose yourselves!'
Francis Carruthers Gould, *Westminster Gazette*, 18 September 1900

A Bogy Score
Mr C.: 'Ha! I wonder what I'd have done without you!'
Francis Carruthers Gould, *Westminster Gazette*, 6 October 1900

Francis Carruthers Gould, Title Page detail,
The Khaki Campaign (1900)

This was also the first General Election in which political cartoons were used widely as a weapon. As Francis Carruthers Gould of the *Westminster Gazette* says in the preface to his cartoon collection, *The Khaki Campaign* (1900): 'At no previous General Election have political cartoons been used so freely, both as leaflets and posters, as during the one just concluded. The fact that both sides have made so large a use of pictorial attacks, arguments, and appeals, shows that the picture has come to have practical value in political warfare.' Gould himself was a fervent Liberal supporter (Lord Rosebery once described him as 'one of the most remarkable assets of the Liberal Party') and he was later knighted for his services to the party after the Liberal victory of 1906.

In 'Political Slimness' (which was also reproduced in colour as a Liberal Party campaign poster) seen cowering behind British Army chief Lord Roberts are Lord Salisbury (Conservative Prime Minister), Joseph Chamberlain (Colonial Secretary), Arthur Balfour (First Lord of the Treasury and Leader of the House of Commons), Lord Lansdowne (Minister of War), George Goschen (Admiralty) and Sir Matthew White Ridley (Home Secretary). The result was a Conservative victory largely by playing on

Brodwick, Minister of War at the Moment of the Signature of Peace
Leal da Camara, *L'Assiette au Beurre* (Paris), 28 June 1902

the Kruger bogeyman with posters claiming that 'to Vote for Liberal is a vote to the Boer'. (The Conservatives were returned to power with a majority of 134 seats.)

One of the new Cabinet appointments following the Khaki Election was William St John Brodrick (misspelt in this French cartoon) – later 9th Viscount and 1st Earl of Midleton – who succeeded Lord Lansdowne (who had become Foreign Secretary) as war minister. He introduced many reforms but was best known to the British public for introducing a new kind of forage cap for the Brigade of Guards, which was named after him.

The Khaki Election also saw the first political appointment of the 27-year-old Winston Churchill who became Unionist MP for Oldham, Lancashire. The son of Lord Randolph Churchill (a former Chancellor of the Exchequer and Leader of the House of Commons) and a direct descendant of the Duke of Marlborough, he had served as a cavalry officer in India, Egypt and the Sudan. A correspondent for the *Morning Post* during the Boer War, he had been captured when the Boers attacked the armoured train he was on and imprisoned in Pretoria but managed to escape and became an overnight hero. His book about his exploits, *London to Ladysmith Via Pretoria*, was published soon afterwards.

The 'Spy' portrait shown here was drawn just before he stood as a Tory candidate for the Khaki Election and the artist has drawn him in the same pose for *Vanity Fair* that he drew his father in 1880 at roughly the same age (Randolph was 31, Winston was 27).

Winston
'Spy' (Leslie Ward), *Vanity Fair*, 27 September 1900

A Nation's Tribute, Love and Tears
John Proctor, *Moonshine*, 2 February 1901

On 22 January 1901 Queen Victoria died, the longest-serving British monarch in history. She was succeeded by the overweight and profligate Edward VII who was much lampooned by the foreign press for his peccadilloes. The drawing by Jean Veber *(below left)* showing Edward's face on the naked bottom of a lascivious Britannia caused such offence that Edward threatened to refuse to open an exhibition in Paris and it was later reissued *(below right)* with blue underwear covering his face.

Shameless Albion
Jean Veber, *L'Assiette Au Beurre* (Paris), 28 September 1901

The Last of the Kings of England and the last Mule of Spion Kop
Leal da Camara, *L'Assiette Au Beurre* (Paris), 2 May 1903

King of England, Emperor of India
Charles Léandre, *Le Rire* (Paris), 2 February 1901

Edward the Fat
Gustav Brandt, *Kladderadatsch* (Berlin), 1901

Chamberlain's Christmas Surprise
'Henriot' (Henri Maigrot), *Le Charivari* (Paris), December 1900

Poor Kitchener
Gustav Brandt, *Kladderadatsch* (Berlin), 1901

Poor Roberts!
What the poor man has to carry in his old age!
F.B., *Nebelspalter* (Zurich), March 1901

A Near Approach to Perpetual Motion
J.M.Staniforth, *Western Mail*, 16 January 1901

Chef's Hands Full
J.M.Staniforth, *Western Mail*, January 1901

In November 1900, Lord Roberts – believing his task to be finished – sent a cable to the British government saying: 'The war is practically over' and sailed from South Africa for England, leaving Kitchener to 'mop up'. Unfortunately this proved not to be the case. A rebellion of Boers in Cape Colony broke out the same month and in December at the Battle of Nooitgedacht in the Transvaal, General Jacobus de la Rey inflicted severe losses on the British. Kitchener soon found himself with his hands full as other rebellions broke out in the region and losses mounted. Guerrilla warfare now took over and Kitchener and his 'flying columns' were kept busy by small groups of Boers known as 'commandos'. Unused to this kind of highly mobile warfare the British troops soon became exhausted.

The Record Catch
The Ratcatcher: 'Eight hundred and twenty-nine! That's the best week's
work I have done yet!'
J.M.Staniforth, *Western Mail*, 14 August 1901

By His Own Noose
Even the art of horse-stealing requires learning
Ludwig Stutz, *Kladderadatsch* (Berlin), December 1900

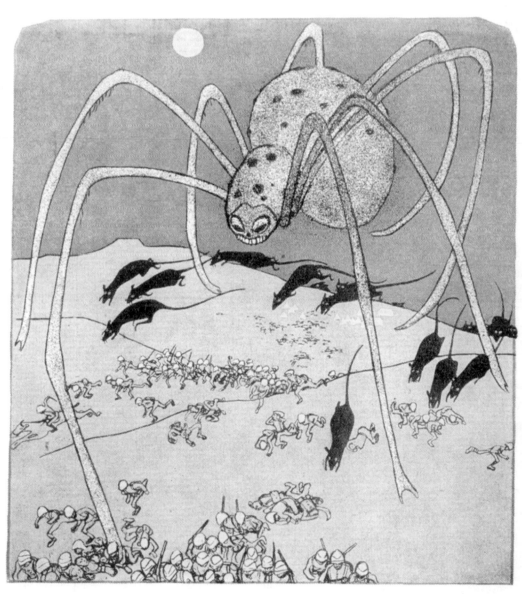

Bruno Paul, *Simplicissimus* (Munich), 1901

On 13 August 1901 Kitchener reported that in a record week's work, his flying columns had accounted for 829 Boers. However, time after time, no sooner had such an announcement of success been made than the Boer forces would retaliate and inflict a major blow on the British.

Staniforth's rat analogy is also used – with the opposite effect – by the German Bruno Paul who has rats, under the command of a giant spider, chasing away the British troops.

Der Völkervielfraß

The People Eater
Kladderadatsch (Berlin), 1901

Such had been the success of the Boers in blowing up railways and harassing British troops that before he left in November 1900 Lord Roberts had issued a proclamation which decreed that any farms found in the vicinity of a train-wrecking episode would be burnt and that prominent Boer supporters would be deliberately exposed to danger by being put on British trains passing though rebellious areas. It is estimated that 30,000 farms were burnt and more than 3 million sheep were slaughtered. This policy, which was continued with increased vigour by Kitchener after the departure of Roberts, was greeted with mixed feeling in Britain and the subsequent actions of British troops were much criticised in the foreign press, especially in France and Germany. Kitchener also introduced a chain of fortified blockhouses, linked by barbed wire and trenches, so that whole sections of the countryside could be cleared. Eventually there were 8000 blockhouses manned by 50,000 troops and stretching 3700 miles.

British Gallantry
Jean Veber, *L'Assiette au Beurre* (Paris), September 1901

English Princesses award the Victoria Cross to the youngest soldier in the army because, though only thirteen years old, he has already raped eight Boer women
Ludwig Thoma, *Der Burenkrieg* (1900)

The increasingly harsh actions by British troops against the Boers in South Africa led to doubts about the veracity of reports reaching the UK, which seemed completely at odds with those described in European papers. Staniforth (*below*) has Dutch, Russian and German men enjoying reading about British disasters at Ladysmith and elsewhere as reported in the Russian paper *Novoe Vremya* ('New Times', 1868-1917). In the German cartoon from *Kladderadatsch* (*right*), the naked Truth holds a looking-glass which has the words 'You You' written on it. There are also references to Pontius Pilate and the Kruger Telegram (in which Kaiser Wilhelm congratulated Kruger on repulsing the Jameson Raid) which the British had regarded as an 'Unfriendly Act'.

What is Truth?
For Pilate it is an open question – For John Bull an Unfriendly Act
Ernst Retemeyer, *Kladderadatsch* (Berlin), 1901

Good News from the War
J.M.Staniforth, *Western Mail*, 4 November 1899

De Wet o' de Wisp
Linley Sambourne, *Punch*, 19 December 1900

Scenting De Wet
W.F.Thomas, *Ally Sloper's Half Holiday*, c.1900

De Wet
'EBN' (Eardley Norton), *Vanity Fair*, 31 July 1902

Particularly elusive were the two Boer commanders General Christian De Wet (portrayed as a Will o' the Wisp in Sambourne's cartoon, *top left*) and General Louis Botha. Despite concerted efforts by Kitchener, whose cordon of blockhouses around the districts infested with the Boer commandos was slowly tightening, De Wet and other Boer leaders remained at large and the war dragged on into 1902. To make matters worse, on 7 March 1902, Lord Methuen and a large British force were attacked by General De la Rey at Tweebosch near Lichtenburg. After heavy fighting Methuen was captured along with 600 British troops and a large amount of guns and supplies. However, De la Rey did not keep his prisoner – the most senior British commander (and the only general) to be captured in the whole war – but sent him back to the British lines a few days later.

In the cartoon by W.F.Thomas (*top right*), the figure on the horse in the wet is Ally Sloper, a character created by C.H.Ross of *Judy*, who was the main feature of the weekly adult comic *Ally Sloper's Half Holiday* (founded in 1884). So-named because he was always sloping off down an alley to avoid the rent-collector, the character was later drawn by W.G.Baxter and then, when he died in 1888, by W.F.Thomas.

The English general and his chief-of-staff

Unexpected arrival of a Boer shell

The General. "Boy, sweep up the chief-of-staff and send me his assistant."

British Phlegm
Caran d'Ache, French cartoon, c.1900

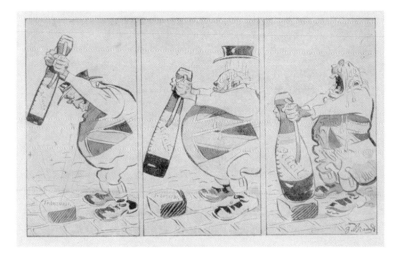

Beyond His Strength?
The English deficit for the last year was almost a million Marks
Gustav Brandt, *Kladderadatsch* (Berlin), 1902

The Dance with Bellona Continues
1. Two months; 2. A year;
3. Two years; 4) Who knows how long?
Gustav Brandt, *Kladderadatsch* (Berlin), 1901

The Lion of the Transvaal
Ludwig Stutz, *Kladderadatsch* (Berlin), 1902

As the uncertainty of the war continued the costs to Britain also continued to rise, not only in financial terms but also with regard to Britain's prestige and honour overseas. In the three cartoons from the Berlin weekly *Kladderadatsch*, John Bull is seen in increasingly frustrating circumstances. In the first (*top right*) – dancing with Bellona, the Roman goddess of war – he gets thinner and thinner as the years pass. In the second (*above*) he is desperately trying to force the paving block marked 'Transvaal' into the roadway with an ever bigger hammer. And in the third (*right*) he looks down on the British lion of Transvaal with a bayonet wound in its side still grasping the laurels of victory as it lies dead on the words 'Glory' and 'Honour'.

English Concentration Camps
'The Blood keeps spurting out – this
rabble will make my crown dirty!'
Bruno Paul,
Simplicissimus (Munich), 1901

In a further attempt to combat the Boer guerrillas – who hid amongst farms and homesteads and made it difficult for the British to identify who was their enemy and who was not – it was decided to collect the population (men, women and children, Boers and native Africans), into what were known as 'concentration camps'. The Spanish had used this tactic against insurrections in Cuba in 1896 and similar camps were also used by the USA in the wars in the Philippines in 1900-1902.

Lord Kitchener introduced the system to South Africa and by October 1901 there were 118,000 European and 43,000 Black South Africans in the concentration camps which were run by the army. However, though by no means as appalling as the Nazi and Stalinist death camps of the Second World War, there was considerable

**Lord Kitchener the Pacifier –
A Job Done and Done Well**
Leal da Camara, *L'Assiette au Beurre* (Paris), 28 June 1902

Lord Kitchener
Jean Veber, *L'Assiette au Beurre* (Paris), 28 September 1901

criticism of the practice both at home and abroad and an estimated 20-26,000 women and children died while in custody, mostly of disease. Liberal Party Leader Henry Campbell-Bannerman, a future British Prime Minister, called the camps 'the methods of barbarism' and after being exposed by Emily Hobhouse, a clergyman's daughter, who came out from Britain to see the conditions for herself, the administration of the camps was taken away from the army and given to civilians.

The three cartoons featuring Edward VII show him trampling on civilians in the camps, squashing them like a wine barrel and walking away with Tsar Nicholas II of Russia while Kitchener smokes his pipe. The two separate French drawings of Kitchener show him in the guise of odious beasts – as a toad and as a wolf or jackal.

S. M. ÉDOUARD VII, Roi d'Angleterre, Empereur des Indes

Le Foudre de Guerre

The Thunderbolt of War
Jean Veber, *L'Assiette au Beurre* (Paris), 28 September 1901

The Allies' Culture Mission
Frantisek Kupka, French cartoon, 1901

155

A Voice in the Wilderness
J.M.Staniforth, *Western Mail*, 24 November 1899

A Good Use for Pro-Boers
J.M.Staniforth, *Western Mail*, 23 September 1901

A Pushing Q.

HERE's our English Quixote Stead,
Brick walls magnetise his head;
You would think it must be dull
Butting brick walls with one's skull;
But he loves it, therefore Stead
Suffers from a swollen head.

(17)

A Pushing Q
Francis Carruthers Gould in Harold Begbie,
The Struwwelpeter Alphabet (1900)

'Lest We Forget'
British postcard based on a *Daily Express* cartoon, December 1901

156

The Two Artists
J.M.Staniforth, *Western Mail*, 31 October 1901

Her Worst Enemy
Peace: **'You make such a noise they can't hear my voice.'**
Linley Sambourne, *Punch*, 11 December 1901

Despite the jingoism of much of the population, it should not be forgotten that there was a large body of opinion in Britain which had considerable sympathy with the Boer standpoint and were against the war. Amongst these were a number of Liberal Party politicians such as Sir William Harcourt (a former Chancellor and Leader of the House of Commons) who said the war was 'unjust and engineered' and David Lloyd George (later Liberal Prime Minister during the First World War) who called it 'a war of plunder'. Meetings were held across Britain and often ended in scuffles with pro-war protesters. Perhaps the most prominent pro-Boer sympathiser in Britain (though ironically a former supporter of Rhodes) was the journalist W.T.Stead, editor of the influential London daily evening paper, the *Pall Mall Gazette*. He also inaugurated a Peace Crusade, founded a journal *War Against War* whose sole object was to stop the war, and petitioned Queen Victoria and Tsar Nicholas themselves. Gould (*opposite, top right*) depicts Stead as Cervantes' Don Quixote on a wooden horse (note the Rhodes and Kruger medallions).

In February 1901 a Proclamation, signed by De Wet and Steyn, was found on a captured Boer and claimed that the British had violated the Hague Convention, had armed Kaffirs (local native Africans) and had violated Boer women and children. This and other reports of alleged British atrocities in South Africa led to a resurgence in activity by anti-war and pro-Boer factions in Britain. Lloyd George had to escape disguised as a policeman after riots broke out during a pro-Boer meeting bravely held in Birmingham Town Hall (the home town of the pro-war Chamberlain) on 18 December, as is shown in the colour postcard (*opposite, bottom*) adapted from a cartoon published in the *Daily Express*. In 'A Good Use for Pro-Boers' (*opposite, centre*), Lloyd George and W.T.Stead are strapped to a train heading for the former Orange Free State (by then the British-run Orange River Colony), renowned for railway sabotage by Boer guerrillas. In 'The Two Artists' (*above*), Sir Henry Campbell-Bannerman (another future Liberal Prime Minister) paints a British soldier as a barbaric monster while the Conservative Joseph Chamberlain portrays him as being exceptionally polite as he asks the Dutch Boer woman and her son to move to a concentration camp. The *Punch* cartoon (*left*) makes the additional point that members of the anti-war faction were accused of prolonging the war by taking the side of the Boers.

Peace
J.M.Staniforth, *Western Mail*, 1902

Brothers at Last
'After the peace conditions were signed, Boer joined with Briton in singing patriotic songs' –
Central News
J.M.Staniforth, *Western Mail*, 6 June 1902

**John Bull Rewards Tommy Atkins
for War Service**
Ernst Retemeyer, *Kladderadatsch* (Berlin), 1902

The End of the War, or Giving, Giving
Edward VII: 'I've won again...'
Alfred le Petit, *Le Grelot* (Paris), 15 June 1902

In early April 1902 the Boer leaders began peace negotiations in Vereeniging in the Transvaal, 33 miles south of Johannesburg, and eventually hostilities ended with the Treaty of Vereeniging, signed on 31 May 1902. As a result the Transvaal and its neighbouring Boer states became British provinces.

The two British cartoons above celebrate the end of the war and reconciliation between the two sides. However, the German and

French drawings are more cynical. In the cartoon by Le Petit (*above right*) Lord Kitchener, looking like a wild beast, hands over a bound Boer to Edward VII who gives him 1.25 million francs in return as Chamberlain looks on. In the German cartoon (*above left*), the disabled soldier and his penniless family hope to be rewarded by John Bull but discover that his safe only contains crutches.

INDEX

Acknowledgements

Ally Sloper's Half Holiday 152
Amsterdamse Courant 126
The Baillie 29
Big Budget 110, 140
De Amsterdammer 142
Der Floh 135
Figaro 40
Fun 60, 61, 63, 64, 65, 67, 70, 71, 73, 74, 75, 76, 77, 78, 79, 84, 85, 86, 87, 88, 90, 96, 97, 98, 99, 100, 101, 102, 103, 108, 143
Graphic 58
Harper's Weekly 94
Hindi Punch 57
Illustrated Chips 129
Judy 6, 91, 113
Kladderadatsch 36, 110, 118, 120, 124, 130, 131, 132, 133, 147, 148, 149, 150, 151, 153, 158
La Caricature 95, 109, 134, 143
La Reforme 122
L'Assiette au Beurre 114, 118, 131, 134, 145, 146, 147, 150, 154, 155
Le Charivari 92, 122, 148
Le Grelot 93, 128, 158
Le Petit Journal 111, 126
Le Rire 59, 119, 122, 135, 147
L'Illustré Soleil du Dimanche 127
Moonshine 114, 146
Münchener Odinskarte 120
Nebelspalter 110, 148
New York World 129
Novoye Vremya 121
Owl 138
Punch 10, 11, 12, 13, 14, 15, 16, 18, 19, 20, 21, 23, 24, 25, 26, 27, 28, 30, 31, 32, 33, 34, 35, 36, 38, 39, 41, 42, 43, 44, 45, 46, 47, 48, 49, 50, 51, 52, 53, 54, 55, 56, 57, 59, 62, 66, 67, 68, 69, 72, 73, 74, 79, 80, 81, 82, 83, 84, 85, 89, 93, 94, 96, 98, 102, 104, 105, 106, 108, 109, 112, 115, 116, 119, 126, 130, 136, 137, 138, 139, 140, 141, 142, 152, 157
Regiment 125
Simplicissimus 58, 108, 122, 149, 154
South Australian Critic 120
Sydney Bulletin 117
Vanity Fair 29, 62, 66, 79, 100, 107, 115, 131, 141, 145, 152
Western Mail 127, 128, 132, 134, 138, 140, 141, 148, 149, 151, 156, 157, 158
Westminster Budget 117
Westminster Gazette 56, 69, 133, 136, 144